WITH THE HOLY SPIRIT AND WITH FIRE

"I baptize you with water for repentance, but he who is coming after me is mightier than I, whose sandals I am not worthy to carry; he will baptize you with the Holy Spirit and with fire."

St. Matthew 3:11

WITH THE HOLY SPIRIT AND WITH FIRE

by Samuel M. Shoemaker

Word Books, Publisher
Waco, Texas–London, England

TO

Sallie Shoemaker Robinson
and
Helen Dominick Shoemaker

BELOVED DAUGHTERS
AND COMPANIONS IN THE WAY OF THE SPIRIT

WITH THE HOLY SPIRIT AND WITH FIRE

Printed in the United States of America

Library of Congress catalog card number: 60-8136
ISBN 0-87680-986-7

Second Word Paperback Printing—September 1972
Third Word Paperback Printing—December 1973
Fourth Word Paperback Printing—June 1976

CONTENTS

WITH
THE HOLY SPIRIT
AND
WITH FIRE

I cannot but think that the reformation in our day, which I expect to be more deep and searching than that of the sixteenth century, will turn upon the Spirit's presence and life, as that did upon the Justification by the Son.

FREDERICK DENISON MAURICE

INTRODUCTION

More people than ever seem to be aware that we need some personal faith to meet life today. Most of them try to come to it experimentally, rather than by authority, and this is the better approach. But after one has begun to find a personal faith that gives meaning and some security to life, he has to ask himself a difficult question. And this is, What difference should this faith of mine make in a world as full of danger and possibility as ours today? Is my faith merely private, irrelevant in the world situation? Is it like a cozy den where I sit reading and dreaming, while the house is on fire? We find faith in the God who revealed Himself supremely in Christ, we learn to pray, we seek (with varying success) to conform our lives to this faith. But what earthly difference does it all make to what is happening, sometimes with terrible rapidity, in the outside world of social and political events?

Our faith, to be sure, is in a God who has created all things; and the universe must be found ultimately on the side of those who believe in Him and try to follow His will, simply because God is the truth, and the way He has created things is the way things are. However weak as yet the effects of faith, the ground of faith is as solid as granite. If believers were sent into catacombs and underground for centuries, and the number of martyrs were increased even beyond the number who have died for their faith in these fearful recent decades, we should be ultimately on the winning side. God would be no God at all unless ultimately, allowing for man's freedom to disobey, He could bring things out in His own way. But this does not give much comfort in such a time of stress and peril and opportunity as the day in which we live.

Our great need is to relate our personal faith to the world situation, so that it is not a merely personal, private thing. But this seems to imply a wisdom and a force which we do not possess. How can it possibly come about? I have thought much about this. I see, as you do, places and people where God breaks through, where the Great Force that alone can accomplish what is needed makes Himself known and felt. The move must be God's, not man's. If we can hitch our personal faith and activity to the whole work of God in our time, and make it a footnote to His overall will and plan, then and then only will it be relevant, especially as it is associated with many others whom God is inspiring, perhaps in quite different ways. Man cannot do this. Only God can do it.

What we are feeling for, imagining, longing for, really praying for, is a world-wide awakening under the power of the Holy Spirit. This alone would be great enough to meet our needs, to use our resources, and to incorporate our little personal stores of faith in a movement greater than anything the world has ever seen. I cannot but believe that this is what God would like to send upon us. The lack must lie, not in His intentions, but in our vision, dedication and passion. If more of us cared and prayed, this just might happen. Maybe it has begun to happen; for there are many "signs of the times" that are not ominous but hopeful, not filled with forebodings but with promise. But we must begin thinking, caring, and praying in wider and deeper ways. We must seek to leave behind us the littleness of merely private satisfactions in faith, and go on to the largeness of public relevance for faith. We can only bring what we have and offer it to God for His use in an awakening of which He must be the Architect.

During the past year I have come upon a book that might help provide the intellectual framework for this awakening. It is called *Spirit, Son and Father*, and it is written by Dr. Henry

Pitney Van Dusen. It is based on the conviction that "in the faith of the Early Church, the Spirit was a central, perhaps *the* central reality. It was not primarily a conviction for thought, certainly not a matter of instructed dogma. It sprang directly from vivid, commanding, indubitable experience." [1]

This is not a wholly novel nor revolutionary idea. It has been heard before. But one cannot read the Acts and Epistles with this thought in mind, as I have lately been doing, without realizing how much truth it contains. This is the book of a scholar, but a thoughtful layman will find it readable and intelligible. The book did two things for me: first, it helped me to realize afresh that the Holy Spirit alone explains the thing we mean by Christian experience and spiritual power; and second, it caused me to talk with my people again and again about the Holy Spirit, using many of the ideas contained in this present book, and to realize how welcome and refreshing a thing it was for them to hear the Holy Spirit spoken about, not with an annual nod at Pentecost, but for several weeks in succession. It was as if together we were finding and digging a new vein of gold. One can own land with gold in it without mining the gold: we began modestly mining the gold, and are not by any means finished with mining it. There is in the mind and heart of an individual, as in those of larger companies of people, what the New Testament calls a *kairos,* a fullness of time, when something takes fire, comes alive, and begins sparking creative contagion and action.

One knows enough of the history of the Church to realize into what vagaries and excesses the emphasis on the Holy Spirit may lead. One needs constant emphasis on the Lord Christ, and on the Church, to avoid some of these pitfalls. But sometimes the nature of our emphasis on Christ and the Church has been like a weight, holding us back from moving on into a fuller and richer interpretation and experience of the Holy Spirit. We must remember also into what poverty and spiritual destitution the Church has often fallen by neglecting the Holy Spirit, or treating Him as a doctrine only. Great numbers in the churches seem to live on the assumption that once we know

[1] New York: Charles Scribner's Sons, 1958, p. 63.

the content of Christ's theological and moral teaching, we have all we need. But what shall energize these potent and familiar truths, riveting them in our attention, getting them down into our "bones," and claiming our wills in carrying them out into life? This cannot be done by will power: we need help, inspiration, continued and constant. What shall tell us the real meaning and actual application of the Sermon on the Mount in such a day as ours? Many of us are theistic in our beliefs, but humanistic in our expectations that we can carry them out. No wonder so much of our modern religion is overactive, success-minded, threadbare, and frustrated. We lack the dimension of depth. We lack the breeze of the Spirit to fill our sails, and carry us steadily forward across the angry and uncharted seas of our world today.

We need to recall that, again and again, when the fires of the institutional Church burned low, the Spirit has blown upon the embers and recalled the Church to its first vision and its first love. So constant, so inescapable, so essential a part of the Church is this, that Bishop Newbigin reminds us that those bodies that cast emphasis upon this part of Christian experience must be termed a needful part of the whole Church. He says, "Catholicism has laid its primary stress upon the given structure, Protestantism upon the given message. . . . It is necessary, however, to recognize that there is a third stream of Christian tradition . . . its central element is the conviction that the Christian life is a matter of the experienced power and presence of the Holy Spirit today; . . . neither orthodoxy of doctrine nor impeccability of succession can take the place of this: . . . an excessive emphasis upon those immutable elements in the Gospel upon which orthodox Catholicism and Protestantism have concentrated attention may, and in fact often does, result in a Church which is a mere shell, having the form of a Church but not the life; that if we would answer the question 'Where is the Church?', we must ask 'Where is the Holy Spirit recognizably present with power?'"[2] "Recognizably present with power" is a most challenging phrase and test. It would take a theologian with a fine-tooth comb to find the Holy Spirit "rec-

[2] Lesslie Newbigin, *The Household of God* (New York: Friendship Press, 1954), pp. 94-95.

ognizably present with power" in much of our ecclesiastical routine.

Our time is not unique. But I think there was never a more widespread feeling in the Church that, in face of overwhelming responsibilities and staggering opportunities, we are singularly unable to give to the world the hope and faith and love which it most needs. One of the ablest, most converted, most effective men I know in the ministry said to me not long ago that he is thoroughly disillusioned with the organized Church, believes most of what we are doing is beside the mark, thinks the Church is simply not being the Church, and wonders what his course of action should be. He writes:

"My own sense of disturbance grows: a growing rebellion and prophetic judgment are coming alive in me toward the institutionalized mechanical elephant. In the midst of all this, I give thanks for the tradition which I love and which may deliver me from a destructive response to so much blasphemy and encrusted dishonesty and supercilious pettiness. As a Church we are being faithless to God's calling. We have often sold out to the values of our culture. The clergy have become the hired supporters of the institution, and are silenced by our own hunger for status and security. Where are people coming alive in the Spirit? Where is there healing and growth in Christian community? Where is there dedicated service to our world? Where are we doing battle with the evil and unjust structures of our Society? Rather we see proper, respectable, socially and statistically successful, prospering congregations who are often threatened and made angry by asking the above questions.

"As for my own calling in the midst of this, it is, first, a deeper penitence and surrender for my own involvement in this and my faithlessness. Second, it is to stay right where I am for now and continue to be a channel of God's renewal of His Church in this congregation. Third, to pray and seek to discover my calling and prepare myself for it. I have grave questions about the validity of the professional clergy—in many ways they seem to be the major obstacle. My critique runs the gamut of local and larger church organization, of theological education, of our present theology, and our irrelevance to the world. I am beginning to feel that there may be a better way to bring leverage on the

Church and clergy than my present vocation allows. Ordination as we now practice it is invalid—the clergy are ordained into separation and the Body of Christ is rifted.

"My own sense of God's grace and love has never been fuller. I love God more than ever and have deeper conviction than before about my calling to be a minister of Jesus Christ. I have a great sense of adventure—that my boats are burned and that I am being led by the Spirit of God into new, strange, and dynamic paths. The death of the old order is painful and slow, but the freedom, openness, and expectancy—the inrush of life—is intoxicating. I give thanks! Pray that I may be faithful here!"

He is not more radical nor upset than some of his fellows in the ministry: he is just more honest. Something tremendous needs to happen to us who are in the Church—all of us. Dr. Paul Tillich has said, "The usual question, 'What shall we do?' must be answered with the unusual question, 'Whence can we receive?' People must understand again that one cannot do much without having received much. Religion is, first, an open hand to receive a gift and, second, an acting hand to distribute gifts." [3] Surely the greatest gift of the Risen Christ to His people forever was the gift of the Holy Spirit. Yet many of us live in a spiritual era that precedes even the Resurrection, let alone Pentecost. We have not come through the two most powerful stages of the Early Church.

I have written this book and sought its publication with many misgivings. It is difficult to make one's meaning clear in the matter of the Holy Spirit. Words reveal, but words also mislead, as one who has been preaching as long as I have comes to know. Moreover, words may freeze truth—and the most orthodox will test them by how tightly they freeze it—but how can one freeze truth about the Holy Spirit? Unless these words take wing and get above the ground of mere statement, they might better not have been written. I want them to be more suggestive than dogmatic, more provocative than final, more directed toward experience than toward theology. I shall say some things about living in the "stream of the Holy Spirit." I profoundly believe this is the native climate for a Christian, as much as water is the natural

[3] *The Protestant Era,* p. 188.

element for a fish. I do not always live in that stream myself—I get out of it, way out of it sometimes. I do not know anybody, even among those who greatly believe in the Holy Spirit, that does not at times fail to live within His stream of life and power. If he says he does not fail in this way, we may be pardoned for suggesting he may be guilty of what Sir Winston Churchill once called a "terminological inexactitude." But I know there *is* such a stream. At times I have been in it. I pray to stay in it more constantly. For the hours when one lives in the stream of the Holy Spirit are the creative, energized, almost miraculous times when one knows firsthand the power of the Living God, flowing in and through him.

This living in the stream of the Spirit is not a special occupation for very holy people. It must be the constant aim and increasingly the experience of every ordinary Christian. There are men and women in professions and business, in hospitals and mills, that come about as near to living in the stream of the Spirit as any people I know. I write this book to encourage them, and if possible increase the number of them. It is meant for laymen as well as clergy. It is written primarily from an experimental rather than a theological angle, though of course there is theology in it, and such—I hope—as is not too inconsistent with the scholars' conclusions. But those same scholars' conclusions must reach the ordinary man in a form more easily digested and calculated to make practical difference in his actual thought and living.

So much real nonsense has been talked about the Holy Spirit by some people who scorn education, and so much is missing from churches that mention Him only theologically or preach about Him at one season of the year, that I think someone must try to talk sense about the Holy Spirit, avoiding the extremes of a pedestrian Christianity that leaves Him out of practical life, or of an excessive emphasis on experiences that seem merely strange and bizarre. This is what I have attempted to do in this book. It may seem incredibly naïve and bold to attempt to write such a book at all, especially to spell out what might be the result of a new discovery of the Holy Spirit as I have sought to do in the chapter on "The New Reformation." The shape of things under an awakening by the Spirit of God can lie only in the mind of God Himself. I think there is something genuinely blasphemous when some of our theologians tell a man like Billy Graham exactly what should be the immediate social effects of his message, forgetful that it took many years before Wesley's movement had its full effect in social areas—forgetful, too, that these critics have been none too successful in turning their own words into experience for most laymen. We need a great faith toward God, a great appreciation toward what others are doing in His Name, and a great humility about ourselves.

Two things have given me courage to go ahead with this book: first, I think that what the book *envisages* is what both the world and the Church most need; and second, while the world-wide scope of such an answer would be unique, there have been in the past, and there are today, signs of "break-through" which may be taken as local patterns of this wider awakening. So many in the churches all over the world are longing, praying, and working for world-wide awakening. In so many lives and places He is already gloriously at work.

The Holy Spirit was given to the Church, and has never been withdrawn. Our need for Him, and for the awakening which He brings, is mounting by the hour. Nothing else on earth seems to me to matter quite so much as that we attempt to put our lives at His disposal, so that if He wills to use us, we are there to be used.

S. M. S.

"Burnside,"
Stevenson, Maryland

1

Our Situation Today

Let us begin by attempting to make at least a cursory appraisal of our situation in the world today.

The most potent overall fact of our time surely is the confident dynamic of a marching communism, having no faith in God but an infinite faith in itself, and over against this the West, materially strong, having a nominal faith in God but curiously little faith in itself, often confused and hesitant. Some of our hesitancies may well prove to have been wise in the long run if they have avoided or even postponed the unimaginable horror of an atomic war. But there is in the West a failure of nerve that is difficult to account for. Dr. Charles Malik says that the West should be more bold about its beliefs and about declaring the blessings of freedom. But a moment's thought will show us that such boldness cannot come from material strength alone, but only from the faith which grounds our freedom in God. G. K. Chesterton said, "There is no basis for democracy except in a dogma about the divine origin of man." We cannot expect to outdo on its own terms a communism that is without scruple concerning either cruelty or mendacity: but if our freedom is a footnote to our faith, then both are written into the constitution of things; and long-run doubt about the final outcome is out of place. It must be clear to us also that we have concentrated far too much on the freedom, which is derivative; and far too little on the faith, which is fundamental.

It appears that, looked at with an eye to the future, the most important nations of the world are the still free but underdeveloped countries of Southern Asia and Africa. They have not often liked what they saw in the West, but Hungary and Tibet are causing them to do some grave thinking about the benefits of communism. We must understand the hesitancy of India to line up unequivocally with the West. But these vast regions with their sprawling and ever-increasing populations now know that, through modern technical skills, there is every possibility for them to "come up" in the world, to use Dr. Frank Laubach's phrase. They want and need the help. From whom will they receive it? Communism has its tens of thousands of trained agents ready to offer assistance—at a price. If the West will offer cooperative help in sufficient amounts, we shall do both our Christian duty by these people and also draw them in the direction of free rather than coerced society. But so much depends on the spirit in which the help is offered. If General Romulo was right when he said, somewhere around 1957, that "we have three years in which to save Asia," then we shall need everything that foundations, corporations, missions, and other private agencies, as well as government, can do to accomplish this huge and pressing task. But a man who has known intimately the workings of government assistance has said that, of the carefully screened people sent abroad to carry out our foreign aid program, only one in four has anything personally to give to the people in these countries. The actual technical help is one thing, and a very important thing; but possibly of even more importance is the "intangible" of courtesy, appreciation, and understanding in the personal relations between our representatives and the people among whom they work.

This is why such work as that of World Neighbors [1] is of such supreme importance. Not only can the work be done for a great deal less money, by working largely through native leadership, but in such private efforts there is clearly no ulterior motive, no ax to grind. This is not relief, this is technical self-

[1] World Neighbors, Inc., 1145 Nineteenth St., N.W., Washington 6, D.C.

help, given at the local rural or village level. It may well be that to package our Christianity in service to the immediate human needs of the people to whom we go is the very best way to commend to them the Christ in whose name and spirit we go to them at all. With the upsurging of native religions today, it could come about that this is the only kind of work Westerners are allowed to do.

It seems quite clear that either some of us in Western lands will go to these people with the essential means of self-help, or they will have to seek them elsewhere. Russia seems fully aware of this situation, far more so than we are. America must appear to many as a prosperous suburb surrounded with blighted areas —and this just can't go on. The underdeveloped parts of the world must have a chance to advance; and if they do not advance with our help in an evolutionary way, they may advance with the proddings of communism in a revolutionary way. But they are going to advance. Some people in America do not see this, and are even averse to sending such help. How stupid can we be? The exclusive pursuit of immediate success in business completely obscures from the minds of many of our people the obvious fact that, if nuclear war should come, and if Russia should prove sufficiently powerful to impose her way of life upon most of the world, there will be no such thing as the free enterprise which we now know. Do they not see that some reasonable unselfishness exercised now might in the end prove to be the very best thing for America and for American business? Personally I have never seen a time nor a situation in which Christian responsibility and enlightened self-interest ran so completely down the same trail!

But what do we Americans do under these circumstances? We have been treated, as someone has said, to a "ringside seat at the Day of Judgment." Some of us recoil from disturbing headlines, go to the office and either pursue the old job in the old way or try to think up bigger, faster ways of doing it. Some of us spend our leisure time mostly as spectators hanging on the radio or television. It is estimated that during one week early in 1959, 72.3 per cent of our 124,051,000 people over twelve years of age spent one billion, eight hundred and seventy million, seven hundred thousand hours watching television! It is our new narcotic. Some of us, failing to do what we should in the world in which we live, set out to conquer space. A Swiss journalist says that "America is striving to win power over the sum total of things. . . . The stake is higher than dictators' seats. . . . To occupy God's place, to repeat his deeds, to re-create and organize a man-made cosmos according to man-made laws of reason, foresight and efficiency: that is America's ultimate objective."[2] I do not know that we should try to turn back the hands of the scientific clock, or whether we could if we would; but I do think we ought to be busier lifting and helping the world of men about us than in the conquest of space.

The real trouble is that America is split down the middle. Some of us are actually as materialistic as any Communist, and have no idea of the spiritual roots of the freedom we enjoy. We want the fruit, which is liberty: we ignore the root, which is faith. A very small minority of our people see the issue clearly, though that minority is growing. Most Americans prefer not to think at all. Between these two groups runs a broad band made up of people who try to be decent, dependable citizens, with no spiritual moorings; and another group that maintains spiritual connections, mostly of an institutional sort with only the most private implications. Only a very small number of Americans realize that faith is freedom's only guarantee—for the God who gave man the courage to seek freedom can alone give him control so as not to misuse it—and that business and the professions and politics are the layman's field for spiritual operations, and his opportunity to manifest his faith at the level of his daily life. We must somehow reach into the company of decent but spiritually unoriented folk, and into the company of spiritually oriented but unmobilized folk, and call out a fresh army of changed and trained men and women who will engage in a spiritual warfare in the world that will match and outdo communism's dreadful power to call out the hidden powers of self-centered people and enlist them in a world-wide cause.

We delude ourselves into thinking that we have discovered a formula for perpetual progress and prosperity. We forget that

[2] Robert Jungk, quoted in *Christianity Today*, Oct. 13, 1958.

prosperity breeds its own self-destroying properties, unless these are continually counteracted by some higher motivations and injections of spiritual responsibility. The late H. W. Prentis, Jr., chairman of the board of the Armstrong Cork Co., said some years ago that we travel in a kind of cycle which runs something like this: "From bondage to spiritual faith, from spiritual faith to courage, from courage to freedom, from freedom to a measure of physical abundance, from abundance to selfishness, from selfishness to complacency, from complacency to apathy, from apathy to fear, from fear to dependency, from dependency back again to bondage." It is not hard to see about where we are in that cycle. Modern man has not beaten that cycle, for all his technical knowledge: for moral laws are higher, more pervasive, and no less inexorable, than physical laws. If we are not to slide all the way down into greater dependency and bondage, we need spiritual awakening.

Men must have some kind of faith to offer them a framework for living. There can be no question that one reason for the rise of communism has been the decline of traditional faith. Barbara Ward has written, "When disturbances as shattering as the 1929 depression strike society, the forces and issues involved are too vast to be unraveled by everyday processes of thought. Men have to revert to generalizations and myths in order to think about them at all. Hence the attractiveness of Marxism, with its apparent power to put every phenomenon into its proper place in a total explanation of man, society, history, human destiny, and ultimate salvation."[3] Theoretically, of course, the possible views of life and human arrangements are numberless, but it looks today as if only Christianity and communism were seriously in the running as forces that can capture men's minds and loyalties. We know that if ever our technical so-called civilization makes a philosophy out of its own discovered techniques, the end results will greatly resemble what communism is already saying. Therefore, whatever our personal preferences for religion or no religion, we had better realize that human individuality, dignity, and freedom will survive only if Christianity itself survives. It is to the interest of every single soul on earth who loves freedom

[3] *Faith and Freedom*, p. 212.

that Christianity should survive; and in part its survival depends on him.

For in the end we all have to reckon, not alone with communism and inflation and nuclear energy and space travel, but with those far more personal factors which nestle not very far out of sight in the inner hearts of us all. Dr. Tillich speaks of "the three gray figures: emptiness, guilt, death." [4] Does life itself mean anything; and if so, what? What can be done about the havoc each of us has wrought in his own small world? And when the end comes, is it the final end? No man of himself has the wisdom to answer these haunting questions, nor the power permanently to thrust them from his mind. Whatever our material accomplishments, though we should draw the distant stars into a neighborhood, we shall go on asking the personal questions about life. And, as faith in God alone offers any real and satisfying answers to them, men will go on believing, not only because belief adds so immeasurably to the richness and meaning of life, but because its opposite turns the universe into what Gamaliel Bradford once called "a wilderness of barren horror."

To the Church has been given the high and ardent task of carrying the flame of faith from generation to generation. We must not expect a perfect performance from the Church—it is too much filled with people like you and me, not changed and converted all the way through, still only in the process of it. But, for all the inevitable human alloy, there is "that of God" in the Church, and it is this which has kept the gates of hell from prevailing altogether against it. We shall be saying later that the Lord of the Church and His Holy Spirit hold the one real answer for our time. But we must be honest about the Church as we are honest about the world, for the Church is part of the world—part of the problem, as well as charged with the message which is the cure.

Father Trevor Huddleston says, "The issue of our day is the issue of communicating to a pagan, post-Christian world: a world which has heard a language and relegated it to the four walls of a Church; a world which will only hear that language again if it can come with a freshness, a stimulus, a shining sparkle." [5]

[4] *The New Being*, p. 102.
[5] Quoted in *Christianity and Crisis*, March 2, 1959.

It is a question whether the "organized Church" as most of us know it can cut short its scholarly, ponderous, long pronouncements, and speak with "freshness, stimulus, and shining sparkle." The Church today is terribly occupied with its own institutional life and immediate success, and it has perhaps given too many hostages to contemporary culture, to say anything crisp and original. We need first a vanguard of spiritually awakened and contagious folk. But this vanguard must never get severed from the organized Church, even when it may more truly represent the Church as Christ wanted and founded it, than does the organized Church. And this for three reasons: first, fresh spiritual impulses usually start with people whose fires have been lit at the ancient candle of faith which the Church carries; second, the Church may be learning through the centuries that it is wiser to foster and protect these small spiritual uprisings than to extinguish them, though there are always glaring instances of the contrary; and third, the Church must offer spiritual nurture and training to those who may be touched and brought to faith by the fresh uprising. The old Church needs the new fire of fresh awakening. The fresh awakening needs the breadth and wisdom of the ancient Church. *Both* are the Church, really. The organized Church cannot stand back in pride and wait to be sought and courted by the new movements, as if they were upstarts and she were the authentic thing: this is pride and cuts off the power of the Spirit. Neither can the fresh movement go on alone, critical and indifferent to the Church, as if it were now the authentic thing and the old organized Church outworn: this, too, is pride and cuts off the power of the Spirit. They have something for each other. I believe they are two sides of the same shield. The mark of the true Church is always the presence and power of the Holy Spirit.

What lies ahead? No man knows. Perhaps we have had our time, and may be near the end of it. We have used it selfishly and shortsightedly. We have been concerned with comfort, pleasure, self. In time of peace we did not prepare for spiritual war: we prepared for more comfort, more rights, more money. We of the nominally Christian West have not shared our blessings, either of liberty, or of faith, with the rest of the world, while we had the time. Maybe the time has passed. There are some good reasons for thinking that this is so.

But maybe there is yet time to shift our gears, to awaken to the situation in the world, to go for helping the underprivileged peoples in a big way, and at the same time go for the winning of America's pagan millions to the Christ whom they should be thanking and obeying. These, I think, are the twin tasks of equal importance which are intimately related to each other. It will take all we've got. No man is indispensable, but everybody is important enough to be under obligation to give his best and his most. Everyone that has anything to give ought to give it—money, houseroom, work, clothes, blood, nursing care, prayer, counsel, faith, love. Only in America is there material plenty. Only as here we discover spiritual plenty also shall we be saved from dying of our riches. Man must put himself at God's disposal as never before.

But man cannot initiate the motion of spiritual power that will take us forward. That must come from the Holy Spirit of God Himself.

2

The Experience of the Holy Spirit

No one who reads the story of the early Christian Church can fail to realize that something tremendous must have happened to this little company for them to begin changing the course of human history. They were led to believe in the resurrection of Jesus Christ from the grave, and in His nature as being one with God. But the experience which empowered them to do what no other group in all the long human story has done went beyond these beliefs, strong and powerful as they were. At Pentecost the power of God descended upon them in mighty force, and we may say that the world has never quite been the same since.

We read in Acts 2 that they were "gathered together with one accord in one place." Gathering in one place is a mere geographical matter: warring armies gather in one region. But gathering "with one accord" in one place is a matter of spiritual achievement. We may be sure that what gave them this measure of accord was their common sure faith in Jesus and His risen life in their midst. Not only did they believe in Him, they were dedicated to His ends and purposes in the world. They were not yet, nor would they ever be, perfect men without divisions in their midst. But they were sufficiently convinced about Christ, and given to carrying out His commands, so that there was a preparation for the fulfillment of His promise that He would send the Holy Spirit to them.

The figures used to describe what happened at Pentecost are those of fire and wind. "The sound as of a rushing mighty wind" was audible to them. The "tongues of fire" that "sat upon each of them" were visible to them. The Spirit usually makes Himself known to the inward ear or the inward eye. This time the experience was so vivid that they felt the current of air in the room; and saw the tongues of fire. There would be many through the ages, and many today, who could testify to experiences similar to this, where the combination of profound spiritual fellowship and an invasion of the Spirit of God produced an effect so palpable that it took on physical manifestations. The current may be so strong that one can be awed, shaken, moved, energized, and empowered by it. The inspiration may be so authentic that one can almost see the light of illumination as one and then another speaks as moved by the Spirit. Such transcendant degree of power as that at Pentecost few would claim ever to have seen; but power like this is not altogether uncommon. I have seen a company spiritually motivated but still composed of separate entities dissolve into an amazing unself-consciousness, a freedom of utterance, a living experience of the Holy Spirit, which could hardly be missed even by the most skeptical observer.[1]

The effect of the Holy Spirit's presence is hard to describe. What these people are experiencing is sometimes called "emotion." At Pentecost there were those who thought the disciples were drunk. Now there is undoubtedly some emotion and some excitement present in a direct experience of the Holy Spirit; but emotion, as we understand the word, represents too transient a state to describe something which in its effects is abiding—at least the total experience of the Spirit may be abiding, even though the feelings incident to the first knowledge of it may subside. The whole appeal of the Holy Spirit is to the total personality—the mind, the imagination, the will, not the heart only. I wish we had some stronger translation of the Greek

[1] See, for example, Series 1, No. 26, of my "This Week's Word," called "God Did This."

word *pneumatikos* that would give a better description of such an experience.

Whether to a group, or to an individual, I think the experience of the Holy Spirit is made known as a strongly *felt* presence. We may feel the presence of the Creator-Father in some part of creation or all of it. We may feel the presence of the Redeemer-Son in a more personal way still. But I think there is often a *nearness* about the presence of the Holy Spirit, as if He were taking the initiative with us Himself. At rare times this will be so numinous, so charged with a sense of the supernatural, that it will almost frighten us; we shall know beyond all questioning that this is no subjective imagining, but a living presence. It is as if He had business with us. He had not just come, He had come for something. We shall see in a little while what some of this business is. I think He is with us many times when it is not made known to us in such startlingly vivid ways; but let us not push from us the thought that at times He makes Himself unmistakably known by His very presence.

There is almost always associated with the experience of the Holy Spirit the element of power. Henry Drummond said that "in the New Testament alone the Spirit is referred to nearly three hundred times. And the one word with which He is constantly associated is Power." [2] This is not like the physical power of a dynamo—it is power of a different sort. Something comes into our own energies and capacities and expands them. We are laid hold of by Something greater than ourselves. We can face things, create things, accomplish things, that in our own strength would have been impossible. Artists sometimes feel this in a verse or phrase of music or some direction that comes to them, and say that it was "given" to them. The Holy Spirit seems to mix and mingle His power with our own, so that what happens is both a heightening of our own powers, and a gift to us from outside. This is as real and definite as attaching an appliance to an electrical outlet, though of course such a mechanical analogy is not altogether satisfactory.

It is not surprising that at Pentecost the Holy Spirit was manifested in tongues of fire and the rush of wind; or that He is

[2] *The New Evangelism,* p. 139.

represented symbolically both by the dove, and by the red flame of fire. We must use figures and symbols to say the ineffable. Fire characteristically manifests itself in the burst of flame, and in the long, steady glow. Fire warms what is cold, fire illuminates what is dark, fire purifies what is impure. Elton Trueblood says the chief quality of fire is its power to set something else afire. Earth, air, and water remain the same: fire is never the same for even a few seconds. The power and the mobility of the Holy Spirit seem most suggested and symbolized by fire. But we cannot escape the realization that fire also burns, consumes, and destroys. The "one mightier than I," who was to be the Messiah, would baptize with fire; this was "the fire of the Day of Judgment that would purge the body of God's people and consume the sinners." [3] John the Baptist, from whom come these words "with the Holy Spirit and with fire," falls in the genuine tradition of the prophets, and like most of them finds something of doom in any authentic "coming" of God. And however much we may wish to see in these words only the positive and merciful side of God's power, we cannot wholly dissociate from them the ring of judgment. Man always has an option in his relation to God. The Holy Spirit will not be forced upon any of us if we resist Him. But in so doing we cannot eliminate the consequences of our resistance. There is, and I think there is meant to be, something a little terrifying in the use of the word "fire" in connection with the Holy Spirit. To be swept clean by Him, so that nothing of us remained but what was pleasing to Him, would be wonderful; but it would be frightening, too. Perhaps we are right in looking upon the association of "fire" with the Holy Spirit in the light of Pentecost, where the fire was altogether benign. But a real "coming" of the Holy Spirit upon a life, upon a situation, upon a nation, upon mankind, will always be an awesome thing, manifesting God's final omnipotence.

If the words "with fire" mean something more positive and benign to us today than they may have meant to John the Baptist, it is principally due to the intervention of the Cross. There are but two ways to deal with human sin, even for God. One is to punish; and the other is to redeem. Sin cannot be

[3] S. MacLean Gilmour.

overlooked, for it is at bottom mutiny against God. What should God do with the self-caused predicament of man's estrangement from Him? The flaming righteousness of the prophets believed He would exercise His right of Judgment. Not until Christ had come, and died on the Cross, did men learn that God was more eager to redeem than to retaliate. Not only could there be no Pentecost until Jesus was risen from the dead; there could be no rising from the dead until the sin of the world had been dealt with on the Cross. We must learn something from the unfolding of the New Testament events, and retrace them—at least to some extent—in our own experience. The Cross is more than the sign of a good Man dying for His cause. The Cross shows how far God was willing to go in atoning for your sins and mine, and in saving us. We can accept redemption: we certainly cannot achieve it. At times it seems to me the real objective of the Cross is to waken us to that in ourselves which is beyond human cure, so that we shall be reached at the very deepest place of our pride: *then* we shall be open to accept His redemption. It begins in a kind of hopelessness—a cry for help—a desperate need that has been met by a divine remedy. "Grace" is the unmerited mercy of God, given to us when we do not at all deserve it. The Holy Spirit is the Bringer of that grace, which flows from the love of God through the Cross of Christ. The Holy Spirit is inseparable from Grace, and Grace is inseparable from love, God's love for us, and our love for Him; and this love is inseparable from our love for one another. When St. Paul has brilliantly described the "gifts of the Spirit" in I Corinthians 12, he makes a departure to "show a still more excellent way." And that way is the way of love, described in Chapter 13. For the greatest gift of the Holy Spirit is love.

The Christian experience of the Holy Spirit, then, holds more than awesome power and cleansing judgment. For the grace shown forth in the Cross restores and renews the life of man through the continuing work of the Spirit.

There is, for example, the experience which causes the New Testament to speak of Him as "the Comforter." This sounds like somebody saying to us, "There, there—don't cry." The actual word is *paracletos,* and it means one who stands alongside to help. And what He says may be much more like "Come on—get up—you can manage—I'll help you." It is a strong word, not a weak nor soft one. At the times when we are on the right track, and when our intentions are high, and what we need is backing and support, there He is, standing right by our side. Too often we forget this aspect of God, and think He is just watching us critically to catch us out. Even when we miss the best, He is still our Father, who wants the very best from us, but goes on helping us when we fail to reach it. We do as much for one another at our best: surely He is better than we!

Another most important experience of the Holy Spirit is His guidance. Dr. Van Dusen says, "If there be a Living God at all, He must desire to make His will and purposes known to men; and a silent, receptive, expectant consciousness furnishes Him the most favorable condition for the disclosure of His thoughts to the minds of men." He goes on to say that his own "experience has been that, when I did so take up an attitude of open-minded and responsible expectancy, thoughts and ideas and directives often came which subsequent empirical testing validated as the closest approximation to trustworthy divine guidance which is available to us."[4] He also calls the Holy Spirit "the donor of direct and immediate instruction from God, and that leading is toward the new, the unexpected, the mandatory. . . . The Holy Spirit is the never-exhausted discloser of 'new truth'"[5] While it is not always easy to know what God is saying to us, and sometimes very easy to be dogmatic where we feel sure of our own guidance, we may be sure that the calls to the saints to take up God's work throughout the centuries have been received mostly through the guidance of the Holy Spirit. We who ought to be true saints but do not always manage to live in this way are yet often the recipients of God's direction when we honestly seek it, and pray in the words of the old prayer that He may "in all things direct and rule our hearts." The difficult thing about guidance is not the receiving or recognizing of it: it is the truly wanting it, so that we come to God stripped, honest, without pretense. Then He can speak directly.

The great, ever-asked question is: How do you know it is guidance? The first uncertainty is in whether we truly want

[4] *Spirit, Son and Father,* p. vii.
[5] *Ibid.*, p. 59.

to know God's will or want to do our own, and in prayer are only trying to win God's approval on our already made plans. We must try to let go of our own desires and fears, and to want His will. This sort of "neutrality" is the only ground of honesty. We cannot wholly banish either desire or fear, but we can put them to one side in favor of an honest asking for God's mind. Sometimes His guidance is direct, as in words or pictures: sometimes indirect, through circumstances. Dr. John Ellis Large says that we should not always look for "Yes" or "No" answers to prayer, but to watch for God's will through the events that follow our prayer: and I think this most wise counsel. Abraham Lincoln once said, "I am satisfied that, when the Almighty wants me to do, or not to do, a particular thing He finds a way of letting me know it." I think that unless we believe that God has a will, wants to reveal it to us (subject always to our own free will), and can do so in spite of our sins, we do not believe in much of a God. And we are not in business with Him until we are seeking His will in all matters, great and small.

There is such a thing, as we shall see later, as living in the stream of the Spirit. Increasingly we can all live that way if we are determined to do so. The people I know who experience the true adventure of faith are continually seeking and finding meanings, connections, coincidences, and "signs" in events which other people do not see. Carried to certain extremes this can appear like romancing with the Eternal; but true faith always seeks and sees the Hand of God in all events. One can be foolish about this, and some are: but the most foolish of all are those who sever themselves from having such experiences at all. C. S. Lewis tells somewhere of a strong impulse to go to a particular barber on a certain day, and finding a wide-open spiritual opportunity with a man in need. It is in such small but great things that the influences of heaven impinge upon the events of earth.

Then there is the experience of the Holy Spirit predicted by our Lord when He said that the Spirit would "convict the world of sin." The real reason why some of us get such poor guidance, or so little of it, is that we seek direction without being willing to receive conviction first. Unless we let Him remove great roadblocks right in front of our doors, we cannot ask Him to show us the road. He is never at pains to point the road to us, unless we are prepared to walk in it. He never satisfies curiosity merely. When to receive guidance is the same thing as to be pledged to obey it, the guidance is more readily available.This means we must sometimes let ourselves undergo the uncomfortable experience of being convicted of sin. "The Holy Ghost, the Comforter?" Sometimes! But sometimes, "The Holy Ghost, the Discomforter." I always feel God takes a practical kind of view of sin, as if saying to us, "Of course you are free to do what you will about this: but if you are going to get into the full stream of My will, and begin doing business in My way, this and this and this are just going to have to be different." Sin is what gets between us and God, or between us and other people, or between them and God—whatever in us creates that situation is sin. Whether this be spending too much money for harmless but unnecessary things (the great American sin in an economy of abundance, when there are thousands in need in our own and other countries), or whether it be persistence in a long-standing resentment or anger, or whether it be some indulgence of the demanding body, until we let go of it we shall not really be asking for God's intervening power. Conviction may have to come before direction.

Another great experience of the Holy Spirit is in being used to bring faith in Christ to another person. One of the most moving stories in the Book of Acts is that of Philip being guided by the Spirit to go down from Jerusalem to Gaza by the desert road; and when he met an Ethiopian eunuch, being told by the Spirit to go and join him as he read in his chariot, (8:26 ff.). The man had been in Jerusalem worshiping, and was reading Isaiah. Philip asked him if he understood what he was reading, and the man said, "How can I unless somebody helps me?" The passage was Isaiah 53, and Philip identified Jesus with this Suffering Servant; and before the day was over the man was baptized as a Christian. Philip did not do this himself: he was used to do it by the Spirit of God. If any of us have been used in this way to make God real to another, we know that we did not do it in our own power. If a person being used in this way begins thinking himself a good spiritual salesman, the power may be taken from him. God uses all kinds of folk to get the message of Himself across to other people—young and old, likely and unlikely. Unless God can use us in this way, it is probable that someone is missing out on finding faith whom we were meant to help. Those who have come to an experience of the Holy Spirit are usually contagious people.

Another great experience of the Holy Spirit is the way He brings unity and fellowship. The world is so full of substitutes for these two great realities that this is a needed discovery today. The early Church was composed of an enormously varied group of men and women. There were sometimes outspoken disagreements in those first days, but I do not think there was any fundamental disunity. This unity above freedom to dissent, above diversity of personality and function, was the work of the Holy Spirit. No other can give this power to "disagree without being disagreeable," this free kind of oneness, this united kind of freedom. When the Holy Spirit comes into a company He begins exerting a quiet inward pressure upon people that lowers the tone of voices, stills the clamor of opinionated convictions, and reminds everyone of the Higher Will that should prevail. When we truly pray in a group, and ask the Holy Spirit to come in on the situation, He lets stand what is sound, He throws out what is merely tempery and willful, and without losing anything that is vital He gives oneness of mind. The Quakers know much of this, and call the unity which becomes apparent "the sense of the meeting." If after waiting prayer disunity of spirit still prevails, it may be God is not yet ready to reveal His next step; or it may be that somebody is just hanging on to his points of view, and this can be real sin. If he will surrender them, he will often find the Holy Spirit putting a bracket over the various viewpoints, the arms of which include something of all viewpoints, and the apex of which points up to Him. I have seen this happen scores of times. Often one has seen little Pentecosts when a group was intent on Christian prayer and planning, and where at a certain point a clear spiritual Force entered the place, with a stir that is reminiscent of Pentecost, and an inspiration markedly like the tongues of fire that day. These are vivid symbols, but not too vivid to indicate very much what may happen. People who work with "group dynamics" may reproduce something that very much resembles the unity of the Spirit, but unless they seek the Spirit consciously and in faith, I think they may mistake the human phenomenon of enjoying the "herd-warmth" of human acquiescence in a psychological trend, for the real unity of the Holy Spirit. This cannot be manipulated.

St. Paul associates the Holy Spirit with varieties of spiritual gifts, in I Corinthians 12, 13 and 14, saying, "To each is given the manifestation of the Spirit for the common good" (12:7, RSV). He lists wisdom, knowledge, faith, healing, miracles, prophecy, distinguishing between spirits, "tongues" and the interpretation of tongues. At the close of the chapter he more or less recapitulates these, noting that not all have all the gifts. He then, in the famous 13th chapter, points to "love" as the great gift and the "more excellent way." In chapter 14, he contrasts the power to speak in tongues, which may edify the speaker but not the hearers, and the power to prophesy, which edifies everybody. We shall have more to say about the meaning of prophecy later on. Suffice it to say here that some kind of utterance, of witness and testimony, seems to have been inseparable from the experience of the Holy Spirit. These people were caught up and were living in a stream of power. I doubt if most of them could have given us a coherent account of who the Holy Spirit is theologically: but they knew Him as an experience. Today we have hundreds of men with trained minds who can tell us all about the Holy Spirit as the Third Person of the Trinity: but do they know Him as an experience? Millions read by incandescent lights who know nothing either of the properties of light nor of how to make an incandescent bulb: light to them is what they see by. This was true of the Holy Spirit at the first. Not theory but experience—not explanation but living power. He was inseparable from what He did, and their knowledge of Him coterminous with their immersion in the Spirit-filled fellowship. You cannot keep light by bottling or boxing it, but only by having it turned on. The Holy Spirit was present only in living power.

It therefore should give us some pause to hear a scholar like Canon Raven say, "Pentecost was the first bestowal of a gift which is thereafter an abiding possession, manifested on many other occasions, though nowhere else so fully described"; [6] or to hear Dr. E. F. Scott say, "At the outset the Spirit was associated

[6] *The Creator Spirit,* p. 238.

wholly with the strange powers which manifested themselves in sudden visions and utterances. For Paul, however, these had become of secondary value. He thinks of the Spirit as an abiding possession by which the Christian is governed in all his thought and action. The whole of the Christian life is life in the Spirit."[7] Both these men use the phrase "an abiding possession." It sounds as if the Holy Spirit were a "thing," like a jewel we could preserve in a strongbox. God's readiness and availability is surely an "abiding possession," but can we say that we "have" the Holy Spirit when we show few of the fruits of the Spirit and almost none of His power? Of course there is a general sense in which He is with and in the Church forever: but it is strange how easily this most fiery aspect of God cools down to ashes when men are not actively, passionately seeking to know and to manifest Him. It is like saying we "have" electricity in the house: but there is no actual heat, light, nor power unless the switch is turned on, is there?

Our next step must be to see what it means to come into the stream of the Spirit, and thus to know Him at firsthand.

[7] *The Nature of the Early Church,* p. 85.

3

Coming into the Stream of the Spirit

How do we conceive of the whole Christian experience, and what picture do we use to think of it concretely? The Christian Faith has intellectual and theological factors in it, and we voice our faith in the Creeds. It has ethical and conduct factors in it, and we often meet it first as a moral challenge. But we know people—indeed we may be people—who have believed in this faith and sought to practice these principles for years, yet nothing specially has happened to us spiritually. These things have not made God real to us, nor made us spiritually contagious nor even spiritually alive. Something is missing. Have we gone far enough to know, not only a Lord who works wonderful miracles and says wonderful words, but who has risen victorious over death? And have we moved on still farther into an experience of the Holy Spirit, such as came to the first Christians?

I like to think of the total Christian experience as coming into a stream of God's love and power. Grace is something that is sent down to us from on high, which we receive by faith. Grace is God's part in all this, faith is ours. Grace is a gift from God. As I write, I am watching the rain come down upon lawns and gardens and fields parched through a month of drought; within a matter of hours what was curled and brown will begin again to straighten out and be green. Grace is like that.

There are several places in the Bible where this picture of the stream is suggested. There is that enormously picturesque verse in Psalm 46, "There is a river, the streams whereof shall make glad the city of God, the holy place of the tabernacle of the most High" (v. 4). There is Jesus' own word about the Holy Spirit in St. John 3, "The wind blows where it wills, and you hear the sound of it, but you do not know whence it comes or whither it goes; so it is with every one who is born of the Spirit" (v. 8, RSV). And there is the picture of the early Church at work, at the very last verse in St. Mark: "They went forth and preached everywhere, while the Lord worked with them and confirmed the message by the signs that attended it" (RSV). None of these suggests a static adherence to a theological belief, nor an effort to live up to a moral code. They suggest a stream of power, like electric, or hydraulic, or pneumatic power, with which one can come into contact so that spiritual events begin to happen. Of course the stream of the Spirit is not impersonal nor physically caused like these; but it is powerful and available like these. The stream of grace is the stream of the Holy Spirit. Lord Elton, in his book *Edward King and Our Times,* says, "What we are disposed to look for in the life of a saint in fact is not so much miracles as interventions, what St. Mark may have meant by 'signs following'"; and adds concerning Bishop King, "When one went about with Brother Edward, one soon came to expect these 'signs followings.'"[1]

How do we come into this stream?

First, I think, we must see some other people who live in it at least for much of the time. Thus we find out that the Holy Spirit and His stream of power are as available today as ever. We may be a little discouraged at first by persons who have so long taken this experience for granted that they have forgotten how they got into the stream, or by the saints who seem obviously so far beyond us. We are often most helped by those who are in the process of getting into the stream themselves. The reason why Alcoholics Anonymous helps so many thousands is that, when an alcoholic, or for that matter any one of the rest of us, goes to one of their meetings, and listens to a man or woman tell of what life used to be like, and how he came in

[1] Pp. 135-36.

touch with A.A., and then how life is now, we realize that this is actual, present-day, available spiritual experience that can come to anyone. Most of us know people who have had some kind of Christian experience. Maybe they are not so very far ahead of us, but they are in touch with power, and we rather envy them. This catches our imagination, and makes us long for what we see happening to them. Imagination lies very close to faith. We visualize something which *might* happen to us. That may be the first step in letting it happen.

Second, we begin making a genuine search. Not long ago I met a man whose spiritual imagination had been whetted, and he had half a dozen books under his arm that he thought would help him in his search. Look for books which not only help to clear the mind, but books that lead right into spiritual experience. People who seek faith go where faith is, as those seeking education go to school or college. Of course we can take a correspondence course in the privacy of our own room if we want to, but it is better to go to school. We may find faith pretty much by ourselves, but most people begin trying the Church again, seeing if it may have something for them. No harm to shop around for awhile, provided we don't become confirmed "sermon-tasters." There are people who are shopping around in every congregation, and woe be to us ministers if we do not remember them, and say something specially pertinent for them—and God have mercy on us if we talk as if all the people before us knew what we are talking about, or were deep in the faith! Begin praying. It may be elementary at first, very doubting, even very selfish. No matter—keep on with it. Jesus' first word to searchers is, "Ask, and it will be given you; seek, and ye shall find; knock, and it shall be opened to you." There is nothing here about starting with a theological belief, and nothing about any requirements whatever: God loves us, and wants to get to us more than we want to get to Him. We reach out to Him in every way we know. And we shall begin to find Him reaching out to us.

Third, try to face whatever is hindering us from finding God and stepping into the stream of power. Most of us seek God because of some need. If we are not troubled about our sins, we are troubled about their effects. Sin may be gross, like drunkenness and adultery and cruelty and hatred. Sin may also be subtle, like wanting our own way and slyly setting out to get it, in home or office or church. Sin is inflexibility and hating to change human plans, even when it is obvious God wants us to do it. Sin is the hesitation that holds us back from jumping into the stream, for fear of how far it may carry us. This is what makes us parsons sometimes talk to congregations about how good it would be to jump in, or tell them the nature of H_2O, or preach pretty little essays on the virtues of bathing. Many of us need to go in very much deeper ourselves. A great deal of our doubt and hesitation is fundamentally fear of letting ourselves go. A friend of mine says that sin is the refusal to be loved by God. We may feel so far from God that we are not "worthy" to seek Him at all. This is to misunderstand God entirely. It is like saying we feared to go to a hospital because we were not healthy enough; or to a college because we were not educated enough. The Church is not a museum, it is a hospital. It is a school, a place for sinners and mixed-up people and beginners. Dr. Charles Clayton Morrison, for many years editor of *The Christian Century,* says that the Church is the only institution in the world, membership in which is based upon unworthiness to be a member. Two high-stepping worldlings dropped into the back of an Episcopal Church just in time to hear the minister say, "We have left undone those things which we ought to have done, and we have done those things which we ought not to have done"; and one of them nudged the other and whispered, "We're in the right place!" God, His Church, and His people are the right place for all of us who know we need help.

Fourth, if we are to step into the stream, we must decide to do it. There is a moment when a swimmer stands poised on a diving board. Maybe the jump is high, maybe the water is cold. Shall we or shan't we? We can't decide to go back when we are in mid-air. It is the dive that matters. It is the dive that tens of thousands of us in the Church have never taken. What we need is a new birth, a conversion. Jesus told Nicodemus he needed it, and Nicodemus was not a pagan nor a beginner, but a learned layman, the kind of person who would have been the leading layman of his Church. Few need to be converted more than eminent clergy and laity. Why? Because pride may beset them all the time. They are "in the know" of spiritual matters, or think they are. What is needed for us all is a decision, clear-cut, definite, with content to it. Dr. Tillich says that "the Christian Gospel is a matter of decision." Archbishop Temple said, ". . . there must be a sharp break. Often indeed a particular conversion takes a long time . . . yet even then its completion takes place at a moment . . . it is in its essential nature abrupt." The longer I think about conversion the more convinced I am that it consists of decision plus growth. We do not convert ourselves: the Grace of God is the primary factor. But we can hold out on the Grace of God, or we can welcome Him in. Our willingness to surrender as much of ourselves as we can to as much of Christ as we understand may be our first step in the experiment of faith. This beginning of self-surrender is our part in our own conversion, and helps to bring us into the stream.

Fifth, it looks as if the early Christians did not differentiate between getting into the stream and staying there through the fellowship of the Church. The personal decision to follow Christ was solidified by being made a member of His company, the Church. When a baby is born, it is normally born into a family: it needs to be fed and cared for, it needs to be trained and taught, it needs to be loved and enjoyed. When a person reaches out for faith with one hand, he will often be found reaching out for fellowship with the other. We want to know and to associate with others who know this same Christ. The Holy Spirit seems able to do His best work in a group. He seems to come more often where a relationship between people has developed into real trust and truthfulness, a kind of openness best described as "love." This cuts down tensions and fears and self-consciousness, with all their short circuits. He comes where there is expectation, flexibility about plans, the easing of fixed viewpoints and stiff attitudes. We need to discover the Church, not alone in formal services, but in informal companies where we can talk and exchange experiences and pray. Some people only find God and come fully into the stream of the Spirit when they see the Spirit at work in a company.

Listen to these words from a university undergraduate concerning his experience in the stream of power: "What a life! Being in God's hands is the most wonderful home imaginable. What a lesson I am learning—do you remember the despondent character of my last few letters? The Lord was teaching me something, that I don't have Christianity, Christ has me. Man, the faithfulness of God! It's the most wonderful revelation. Your letters and books, constant prayer, reading, and fellowship, plus the wonderful power of the Holy Spirit, are all combining to show me so convincingly that God's love is faithful and abiding. I feel great. My girl's roommate just became a Christian. We've been praying for her for almost two years. I saw her last week and she was so hungry. I gave her *How To Become a Christian,* and the Holy Spirit took over. What a thrill! The book is now circulating throughout her college and I am praying for its use. . . . There's nothing in this world more thrilling than talking to people about God. I find that each time I talk with someone, I learn so much that I never knew before. The Lord just uses me, and I sit there and listen." Why are there not more men like this—strong, a fine athlete—being produced by our work in colleges, and our Young People's groups at home?

An older woman with very little money, but a growing, lifelong faith, began to feel that she should go to see some friends who are getting old and needed her, in a country across the ocean. She loves them and their country, and wanted to spend the summer with them, but gave it up. Then came a letter from them, saying, "When are you coming over to see us? Can't you come this summer?" In her listening time with God, she asked realistically, "What shall I do? My savings are getting low. Tell me what You want me to do." The guidance that came to her was, "If you want to go, you can go. The money will be provided for you. Fear not." A little later came a check for three hundred and sixty dollars from a society to which her father (a clergyman) had contributed many years ago, and which exists to help widows and orphans of clergy. A company in her city had overcharged her and they sent back a check for a hundred dollars. And these two items took care of almost the entire expense of the travel to and from the foreign country. She says, "Isn't God kind and faithful?" When someone counters, "But things like that never happen to me," one wants to say: remember that here is a joyously dedicated life, responsible and obedient at many steps along the way, who has provided a receptive vehicle for God's power and whose faith has made possible such an "intervention." This is the kind of thing that happens to this kind of person. But she was not always that kind of person: she had to turn a pretty conventional church religion into a yielded, expectant, witnessing life. After a certain time it seems as if the supernatural is perfectly natural!

Suppose one has known what life in the stream of the Spirit is like, and then for some reason has gotten out of it? Old words about old experiences begin to take the place of fresh words about emerging experiences. What can be done? I heard a man tell of such an experience. A few of his believing friends realized what had happened, and quietly began to pray for him. He went through a few weeks of real estrangement from God, and consequent inner suffering; and this was used as a time of purgation. There was increasing anguish in it, and it began to appear in lessened vitality and health. But prayers were being prayed. He said that little wisps of encouraging guidance began filtering through to him. One Sunday morning he went to the early Communion service, and while there was no unusual emotion at the time, there came a gradual lift afterward. That afternoon, at a social party, a man whom he knew began talking to him: he saw a great change in this man, who began witnessing about how he had fought off real giving-in to God. Recently he had "let go," and already the change was showing up in new moral courage in his conduct of business. Prayer, sacramental grace, and fellowship all had their part in bringing him back into the stream of the Spirit's power. But something of self had also to die again. We do not leap easily into this stream, like a swimmer on a hot day into a cooling stream of water.

Sometimes we wonder why some come into the stream, while others stay out; why some are truly changed, and others not. Perhaps the reason is not far to seek. The "strait gate" and the "narrow way" mean always a bowing of the knee, an inadequacy, a cry of despair, a call for help from God and from others. The trouble with a lot of us is that we have never been broken. We grew up as nice people in the Church, we covered our real sins with pride. We did not dare let ourselves feel desperate. We did not cry out to God in despair—we would carry things through ourselves. Therefore nothing ever really got at our unbroken, still feverish pride. We must somewhere hear the true, convicting Word of the Gospel, sharpened by the Holy Spirit; and unless this has in it enough of what is humanly called "emotion," it may not be able to break through our hard shell; mild church services simply do not accomplish this for a great many of us. There is a death to self in coming into the stream of the Spirit. There will probably need to be more than one such death during our pilgrimage. Many things are given us in the Crucifixion and the Resurrection: but one simple and obvious fact is the inescapable truth that only by death can resurrection take place. That remains as true for us as it was for Him.

4

Reason and the Holy Spirit

It appears as if those who emphasize only the experience of the Holy Spirit, without the use of human reason, fetch up with a concept and a practice that is often so extreme as to make it incomprehensible to people who are accustomed to use their minds. It also appears that those who emphasize only the rational and theological aspects of belief in the Holy Spirit, without corresponding emphasis on experience, wind up with so desiccated and powerless a concept of the Holy Spirit as to make Him virtually a concept only. Can we find an understanding that is dynamic, an experience which is also reasonable? On the whole the more regular churches have made of Him a doctrine, and on the whole the freer denominations have made of Him an excitement. Surely there must be some *via media* between these two extremes.

But how shall we think of Him? We can say words about Him that are true, but these will not necessarily bring people to Him. Perhaps we dare not try to think of Him at all until we have begun to have some experience of Him; for the theoreticians have done as much harm by leaving Him a concept only as the extremists have done by refusing to use their minds. Define Him we cannot—I cannot define you, nor you me—how much less this most creative and original and unpredictable Person of the Trinity? We believe Him to be one with the Father and the

Son, co-equal with Them, coming forth from Them, ever in communion with Them. If we are Christians, we pray almost indiscriminately to the Father, or the Son, or the Holy Spirit. These are three "personae," three modes of manifestation of the same God. There is danger even in saying "three," because we tend to forget that there is but one God. There is also danger in any attempt at definition. Nobody knows the real nature of electricity—Edison didn't, Einstein didn't, though they could channel it to do wizardlike things. We know electricity by its effects, such as heat, power, light. Only so do we really know the Holy Spirit. He is the irregular, creative, completely untrammeled Person of the Trinity. He must resist our efforts to capture Him in any formulas whatever. Try to put electricity in a box! Electricity only *is* what it is *doing*. Just so is the Holy Spirit. You know Him only when He is "on," like electric power. Think of God in His foraging, invading, energizing, vitalizing, renewing, enlightening, convicting, strengthening aspects; and we shall come somewhere near the Holy Spirit. But we must know Him before we can even try to define Him. I dare to say, the experience of Him must always precede any interpretation of Him.

I think of Him as the roving Center of all God's activity in the world. He is the Inspirer of all truth—philosophical, scientific, practical, as well as spiritual. He is the Creator of all beauty, whether it be channeled through worthy or unworthy instruments. We say in the Creed that He "spake by the prophets." Jewish prophets? Yes, of course, but other prophets of other religions with truth in them: for He is the Author of all truth everywhere—it is His to know, and His to dispense. He is in every work of mercy, in every good and gentle life, in every reconciliation between estranged people or groups, in every lift of the spirits of overtaxed and suffering people. In all that good men seem to do, we shall find an Unseen Hand at work, in motivating it and giving grace to carry it through. In the blackest and the worst of men, whatever spark of goodness remains to be touched, it is the Holy Spirit. He is more pervasive than the ether. He is God in His widest, most ingenious, most far-flung aspects. He is God in His most minute and intimate aspects. He is God at work in us and available to us. In His own very gentle way, He is always taking the initiative with us.

Historically He was given supremely to the Early Church by the promise of Jesus, "It is to your advantage that I go away, for if I do not go away, the Counselor will not come to you; but if I go, I will send him to you" (St. John 16:7, RSV). The Resurrection and Ascension of Jesus came first; then the gift of the Holy Spirit. Thereafter it appears that the great, central reality of the Early Church, the universal Successor to the historic Jesus, was the Holy Spirit. We wonder why that Church accomplished so much against such odds. The answer is, the Holy Spirit. We wonder what could set alive for those average people the great riches of the Gospel. The answer is, the Holy Spirit.

We must now consider the relation of the Holy Spirit to Jesus. And we must begin by affirming that, while there seem to be suggestions of the Holy Spirit in the Old Testament, and in other religions, historically the revelation was first the Son, and then the Holy Spirit. Dr. Rufus Jones once called Christ "a complete expression of Divinity and Humanity." The cosmos "had" Jesus, as a mother has a child; and the deeper meaning is that God is exactly like Jesus. Wrought out in terms of a human life, Jesus shows us what God is, and what a life centered in God is. The clear faith of the Early Church was that Jesus is the Christ, and that He is risen from the dead. The blaze of the Resurrection is over all the life of the Church in its first glorious days. The divine and risen Jesus, the near and powerful Spirit, seem workingly almost interchangeable.

Yet it appears that the Holy Spirit took on just where the historic Jesus left off. It appears that the Holy Spirit is Jesus universalized, made timeless, made omnipresent. He was a kind of spiritualized Incarnation, a Christ without physical limitation or trammel. We might say that Jesus made God's nature known, and the Holy Spirit made His power available. Jesus brought Him into the historical area, and the Holy Spirit brought Him into the area of daily experience. It is common to hear Catholic-minded folk say that the Church is the extension of the Incarnation. It is becoming my own conviction that the Holy Spirit is the real extension of the Incarnation; but I also see that He cannot be separated from the life of the Church, either theoretically or practically. He is the Spirit of the continued Incarnation: the

Church is the body of it. But the Church dare not claim to be the extension of the Incarnation, except as she is infused and indwelt by the Holy Spirit. Without this, the body is dead; and no dead body, however once alive, can be an extension of the life of Christ in the world.

There is a frequent turning back to Jesus and relating the Holy Spirit to Him. St. Paul identifies and equates the Two, affirming that "the Lord is the Spirit" (II Cor. 3:17 RSV). He says that ". . . no one speaking by the Spirit of God ever says 'Jesus be cursed!' and no one can say 'Jesus is Lord' except by the Holy Spirit" (I Cor. 12:3, RSV). St. John declares that, "By this you know the Spirit of God: every spirit which confesses that Jesus Christ has come in the flesh is of God, and every spirit which does not confess Jesus is not of God" (I St. John 4:2-3, RSV). These remind us of Jesus' own word about the Holy Spirit, "He will take what is mine and declare it to you" (St. John 16:15 RSV). Clearly Jesus is the anchor and safeguard for a right faith in, and experience of, the Holy Spirit. I knew a man once who came to a profound belief in the Holy Spirit, but who missed altogether any real faith in Christ as divine Lord: and in time this left him confused and without a sufficiently objective anchor for his personal faith and experience. I profoundly believe that a genuine experience of the Holy Spirit will lead us to Christ.

If, as Dr. Van Dusen contends, the faith of the Early Church found the Holy Spirit "*the* central reality," and this was based upon "indubitable experience" (and I have reread the Acts and the Epistles with this contention in mind), I am wondering whether this new generation of believers, who cannot have seen Jesus in the flesh, did not experience Him through the Holy Spirit in the body of the believers, the Church? More and more, I think that they did. What they saw and experienced was a fellowship of people imbued with, and inspired by, the Holy Spirit, working changes and wonders in and through them, carrying on the same kind of things that Christ did when He was here in the body. In a sense there was no difference, only a continuation.

But what this causes us to ask is: Are we exposing people today to the Spirit-filled fellowship as their first acquaintance with Jesus Christ? Some Catholic-minded people will say that this has always been their contention: we truly find Christ only in and through the Church. But I should then want to ask them why there is such a disparity between the Catholic churches and the Early Church—the body is there, but where is the Spirit—the Spirit who did such things as we read about in the Acts and the Epistles? I agree about the need for the body: must not the more Catholic-oriented agree about the need for the Spirit, also? If it is true that in all our churches—Protestant, Catholic, and Orthodox—it happens all too seldom that people come to a living experience of Christ through a Spirit-filled fellowship, must we not alter our ways? Time was when people apparently came to the Holy Spirit through Christ. Has not the time come when many of them might better be brought to Christ through the Holy Spirit? This is not a change in basic theology; but it is a change in emphasis and procedure.

I am convinced that much of our preaching and teaching about Christ misses the mark and does Him a grave disservice. When we do not take people on into a vivid, current experience of the Holy Spirit, we begin putting a wrong kind of emphasis upon Jesus which keeps Him in a familiar and historic and theological corner and does not let Him out of it. We say all the correct and orthodox things about Jesus, in our hymns, our liturgies, and our sermons; but sometimes these do more to conceal than to reveal Him. We make Him ecclesiastical through a heavy-footed emphasis on the Church, rather than upon the Holy Spirit, as His true successor in the world. We make Him sentimental, with the milk-white robes and the sickly-sweet smile. We eulogize Him, when we ought to witness to Him—I have read books and magazine articles, and heard sermons, that almost turned my stomach with heaped-up eulogy and repetitious theological affirmations, which He does not need from us. We embalm Him in proper words of belief, and do away with Him in lip service divorced from immediate and dynamic spiritual experience. We obscure Him in hymns that drip with a kind of sad sentimentality, and express a devotion we do not honestly feel. We make of Him an appendage to our Western culture, instead of realizing that religion is the soul of which culture is the temporary body. Many of the scholars who seek to exalt Him involve Him in their precise and complicated words, so that the common people cannot understand what they say of Him. We lose Him in the maze of religious activity and human service, which might be all right if it stemmed from a real experience of Him. We even make Christ Protestant, and Western, and white! What a travesty is this of the real manifestation of God that was Jesus! How the incubus of all this attaches to almost everything we say about Him! People do not hear the fresh, living, convicting "word" about Him—because the religious conservatives test the "word" by whether it repeats the old theological shibboleths; and the modern-minded ask whether it measures up to the last psychological or technical wrinkle of contemporary trends. Or else people just say it is "old stuff," and they have heard it before, and all the bite has worn off it, like a file too long used on iron. No real speaking about Christ in the power of the Spirit can ever be called "old stuff" by anybody, even the most hardened skeptic. Of course it is not the real Christ that is like any of this, but the terrible things we have done to Him—our wordy arguments that *our* church is better than another—the flat, lackluster faces we wear—the terribly uninspired lives that some of us lead. When we hear a voice that is filled with faith and the Holy Spirit, Jesus comes alive. For many He comes alive when they are brought in touch with the stream of power which is His Holy Spirit at work in individuals and groups and churches today.

Does all this mean that Jesus has had His era, and failed? Nothing of the kind. It means we have obscured Him by doctrines divorced from life, by activities that no longer activate faith in us or in others. It means that often only with difficulty can people find Christ in His Church, because the power that marks His presence is so often missing. It is not that Jesus is worn out: it is that our categories and misrepresentations of Him are worn out. The clergy are just as responsible for this as the people, probably a great deal more so. On the whole, our clergy are giving arguments in favor of religion; and on the whole, our people are busy trying to live up to Christian principles. Both miss the mark. The clergy need to heed the wise words of Lord Lindsay, one-time Master of Balliol College, Oxford: "You ministers are making a mistake. In your pulpits you're arguing for

Christianity. And no one wants your arguments. You ought to be witnessing. Does this thing work? Then share it with the rest of us." It may be that we shall need to be plunged more deeply into the whole of the experience which Christ created through the Holy Spirit, with its attendant events and "signs following," before we can ever see Christ Himself again with any genuine clarity.

Let me follow this thought through in at least two fields where we ought to be making impact and winning people today.

The first is in lands overseas, where Christ is less known and where other religions are in the ascendant. If the Holy Spirit is God at work and seeking entrance into every heart, we shall expect to find Him wherever men admit their need and seek for God, under whatever name. If there be any truth whatever in any religion, He is the Author of it and He put it there. Shall we not make better contact with non-Christian people by recognizing what they already have of the Holy Spirit, rather than by acting as if they had none of Him at all? Dr. Van Dusen tells of visiting a remarkable Christian institution near Hong Kong, called The Buddhist-Christian Institute. It was begun by Scandinavian Lutherans. The Chinese title, Tao Fongshan, means "the hill of the Spirit of Truth" or "the hill of the Word of God." It is a retreat center where Buddhists, especially priests, who want to know more about Christianity can go to study, reflect, and live. They are free to return to Buddhism, or they may remain on. There is a dormitory for preliminary inquirers, and one for those who have decided to become Christians. Above the chapel altar hangs the Star of Bethlehem, and here and there is seen the insignia of the order, an open lotus lily (Buddhist symbol of unfolding truth) above which is a Cross. The two faiths have in common a conception of the Spirit of Truth, or Logos, or Word of God. The Christians look for the fulfillment of the Buddhist belief in a growing faith in the Holy Spirit. This seems a most inspired approach.

The second field is the intelligent, industrious, often good-willed people at home who do not accept the Christian faith. We think we are being loyal to Him when we challenge them directly by stating propositions about Him. Would it not often be much more effective if we made common cause with the light they already have, appreciating the best of what they do, learning their sources of inspiration, and gradually coming to the place where we can talk experientially about our Source of inspiration? Experience is much better than argument, but even experience which too strongly suggests a difference must be brought in with great tact and understanding. Nearly all men believe in what they often call "Something." Of course we want them to go on and identify this with God and with Christ. But when we declare our faith as if it were the last word of truth, we often lose them. Thinking we are being loyal to Christ, we may succeed in being very disloyal to Him, not in intention but in effect. If it is possible to draw such people into a small group of honest, natural, human, seeking people among whom prevails even a trace of that amazing "fellowship of the Holy Spirit," it may do far more than an individual approach may do. This indirect, experimental, group approach may accomplish much more than our dogmatic witness can. People are sometimes brought to Christ through first being brought into contact with the Holy Spirit as He is at work in the lives and in the relationships of others.

What we are saying is that the churches, all of them, need another approach than the common one of presenting Christ. We have spoken of some of the weaknesses of the Catholic way. We must say equally unhappy things about the typical Protestant way. For, as Catholics tend to regard the Holy Spirit as the possession of the Church, not to be found anywhere but in the Church, so Protestants tend to regard the Holy Spirit's presence and power to be found only in the Bible, and in the spoken truth of the Christian message. The one is as confining, as unworthy, as untrue, as the other. The immense rise and growth of what educated churchfolk are disposed to call sects are warnings that God can go outside the organized churches for agents if He needs them. I often have the feeling that the somewhat wild, experimenting mistakes of the spiritually earnest and emotional are actually far more pleasing to God than the prim, self-conscious poses of those in the Church who criticize these things, who sit in elevated seats of the scornful, and manage to provide so little genuine and exciting experience for their fellows. Religion may not be so wild and emotional as these sectfolk make it; but, in the name of God let it be said, religion is not so tame and dull as the conventional churches have succeeded in making it most of the time! There is a chance to learn something from a wholehearted mistake, there is little chance to learn anything for those who will never let themselves go with a passionate earnestness. There can be only an incredible dullness and rectitude in people who have abandoned all enthusiastic search for anything more than the extremely safe and correct rounds to which they have accustomed themselves. Today there may be more spiritual vitality in the sects than in the churches. The needs of our time are great and desperate. Will the overall Church, going at its present rate, be able to overtake the galloping revolutionary forces? Is God's answer for this time a worldwide awakening of the Church and the world by the Holy Spirit? We need every movement, every Church, every life that can be mobilized in this mighty conquest under the generalship of the Holy Spirit. It will not be our ecclesiastical credentials, it may not even be the correctness of our theology, that will put us into the forefront of that battle. It will be the depth of our dedication, and our willingness to be guided and used by the Holy Spirit. The real "lunatic fringe" in this hour may not be the people we call the "crack-pots," but it may be all of us who, though in the churches, are out of the Spirit.

I believe the things that I have been saying, else I should not have said them. Yet I know that, whether one takes a long, historic view, or whether I simply look back into my own life, it is impossible to think of having come to these experiences and conclusions without the God-given and God-ordained instruments of both Church and Bible. These, together with private prayer, have ever been the bulwarks of our faith in the world, and they will continue to be. We are meant to come up through these given "means of grace" to the rich life in the Spirit. The Spirit will throw His light back upon them, so that "the Word" will continue to waken and teach us, so that the Sacraments will continue to feed and sustain us. I think that the experience of the Holy Spirit can grow individualistic and thin when pursued apart from constant absorption of the Word, and constant immersion in the fellowship. But I believe that without the inspiration of the Holy Spirit to speak to us now through the Word, we can make an idol of the Bible; and I believe that without the inspiration of the Holy Spirit living in and through the Church today, we can make an idol of the Church. What are Church and Bible all about? About Jesus Christ, of course, and our relation to Him. But if, after the Ascension, the immediate Hand of His help was withdrawn, and if He meant the Holy Spirit to be His working Surrogate in the world forever after (as I think He did), then our relation to Christ is through the Holy Spirit. If we read our Bibles with the light and inspiration of the Holy Spirit, and if we worked and prayed and worshiped in the Church as if it were truly "the fellowship of the Holy Spirit," the awakening we need would have begun among Christ's believing people. Once it truly began in us, it would spread at once beyond our borders, and the world would know it.

The miracle is that we can be an onlooker or even a skeptic one day, and a participant the next. We can be a churchgoer, and even a nonchurchgoer, one week, and a fisher of men the next. It depends on whether we let the Holy Spirit come in. Any one of us may keep Him out, and any one of us may let Him in. All of us live amid the blessings the Holy Spirit has caused; but we shall never really know Him until we are consciously in contact with Him, and are beginning to be His agents and channels. The Holy Spirit comes again in power through individuals who surrender themselves to Christ and link themselves with others trying to do the same thing. Thus does awakening begin, in the Church and in the world.

To recapitulate: I am convinced that most of us who call ourselves Christians are living far short of our possibilities because, though we give Him the lip service of belief, we do not know the stream of power which is the life of the Holy Spirit today. I am convinced that much of our preaching about Christ consists of well-meant words that lack the authentication which would bring them to life; and that authentication can come only as we ourselves live more profoundly and more consistently in the Spirit. The word message of the Gospel is no more the whole of it than the sacrament-centered practice is the whole of it: both can be out of the life unless there is continuous fresh discovery of the Holy Spirit through the initiative He takes today with His Church—and sometimes clear outside it. Jesus is our Lord and

Savior, the Author and Anchor of everything we are saying about the Holy Spirit: but He certainly commanded us to go forward into the stream of new life which He was going to provide through the coming of the Holy Spirit. The one real test of the reality and validity of the Church and the Bible is the power and presence of the Holy Spirit, directly and personally perceived: belief in inspired writing, or in regularity of origin and operation, is no substitute for this. I believe that the coming of the Holy Spirit made it forever impossible for a true follower of Christ to rest content when he has an exalted view of Jesus' divinity alone, or when he loyally seeks to obey His commandments alone: he must go on into the discovery of the Holy Spirit, as the guarantee of growing experience. I am not sure that the coming of the Holy Spirit was not Christ's way of saying to us that theology and ethics must constantly be backed by experience. This is not an extra: this is part of original and essential Christianity. We who belong to reasonable and educated churches must admit our deficiency and delinquency in this regard, or people in large numbers will continue to turn from us and seek the richer experience elsewhere, like the woman who, when asked by Dean Pope of the Yale Divinity School why she had changed to one of the more primitive sects, replied: "I needed more of the Holy Ghost than the Baptists could give me." [1] We shall help people find Him with reason, or they will begin going after Him without reason: doctrinal orthodoxy alone is not an experience of the Holy Spirit.

[1] Quoted in *Only in America* by Harry Golden, p. 109.

5

The New Reformation

Two things we must never lose sight of: man's plight today, and the power of God. We face in the world the simple issue of extinction or survival. We can now destroy our civilization, perhaps our race, and even our planet. Revolution gallops in three directions: political change, with the decline of the ideals of freedom and the leadership of the West; nuclear discovery, with what bane or blessing to mankind none can foresee; and spiritual demoralization, centered largely in man's deification of himself and his determination to make himself master of the universe. The conflict created by man's new-found powers, and his capacity to destroy everything that matters to him through these same powers, is part of the terrible tension of our day. The most informed and thoughtful men who comment on this odd scene are the most desperate. While man's knowledge increases, his wisdom seems to have come to an end.

Now is the spiritual chance of the ages! The true alternative to an atomic holocaust is a world-wide awakening under the Holy Spirit. To bring this about is outside the capacity of any man or group of men. But it is not beyond our imagination, our prayers, or our hope. It is not beyond the power of God. We have never in history seen anything so vast as this must be; but we have seen local instances of what it should be. Gerald Heard says that the late Harold Laski admitted to him "with a sad shake of the head" that John Wesley prevented singlehanded the French Revolution from coming to England, ". . . one man, an Oxford scholar. He went down and out into the uneducated world to save souls. He cared for men's, individual men's, eternal salvation. And as a by-product, he saved his society, including many who hated him and were indulgent, greedy sinners, from revolutionary destruction." This might be multiplied, spread on a vast scale, if more of us were set free from our denominational prides, our bureaucratic setups, and our preoccupation with small things, and if we began praying for world-wide awakening, and for a share in it, that God's Holy Spirit might blow upon our chaos and give us the awakening we so sorely need.

I believe that many other agencies beside the Church must have their share in this but the Church ought to take the lead. It ought to be the one outfit that is unselfish enough not to care who gets the credit if only the work is done. But we need a new shuffle in the Church. We are chewing very old cud, and in many places fighting for the wrong thing. There needs to be a very great movement of the Spirit, greater than us all, including us all (please God) but transcending us. The old verities in their present setting have a curiously mocking and metallic sound. We need a New Reformation that will go very much farther than did the one of four hundred years ago, and reverse some of its trends. This is the thing we ought to be concerned about, thinking about, praying about, working for, in all the churches—not our trivial church differences and ceremonies—certainly not our absurd trust in the millions of words we say and write in sermons, reports and official pronouncements. These are the things we *say* when we lack the power to *do*. The most voluminous parish report is sometimes that of a parish that is doing nothing but wants to make a show; and the most adequate and ponderous pronouncements come from churches and inter-church groups that can do no better than project a pretentious wish.[1] Unless I can suggest some ways by which ordinary clergy

[1] Since writing this, I have seen Dr. Hendrik Kraemer's comment, in *A Theology of the Laity* (p. 85), on some of the recommendations of the Third World Conference on Faith and Order, Lund, 1952. He says, ". . . if the sovereign *reality* and *claim* of Christ and the Holy Spirit on the Church, her spirit and life, were allowed to become the driving factors in the attempt at self-revision and new obedience, incalculable forces would

and lay people can make their lives and their churches factors in world-wide awakening, this book will be another of the same sort. Bishop Lawrence of Massachusetts used to say that the great American heresy is to think that because a thing has been said it has been done!

We must think in very large terms. The New Reformation must aim to be not only world-wide but universe-wide. Exactly as the men of science in our time think in wholly new dimensions, and in terms of limitless space, so must we. Hear these almost breath-taking words from Tillich: "The function of the bearer of the New Being is not only to save individuals and to transform man's historical existence but to renew the universe. And the assumption is that mankind and individual men are so dependent on the powers of the universe that salvation of the one without the other is unthinkable."[2] This recalls St. Paul's great vision of the final consummation of things: "Then comes the end, when he [Christ] delivers the kingdom to God the Father after destroying every rule and every authority and power. For he must reign until he has put all his enemies under his feet. . . . When all things are subjected to him, then the Son himself will also be subjected to him who put all things under him, that God may be everything to everyone" (I Cor. 15:24-28). If the cosmos is really "creation," then full and final redemption must find its way into its uttermost corners and farthest spaces. Perhaps we shall find life on distant planets, and perhaps that life has not strayed from the will of the Father as we have—we just could be the "black sheep" of the universe. It must be the complete will of the Father that the whole creation obey Him and acknowledge Him and praise Him.

One has the feeling that the New Reformation must strive more and more to let the Spirit of God come into all natural

---

enter which might change a theological commission into a Pentecost. New obedience to Christ and His Spirit, not better theology (unless the theology is the result of a new obedience) is creative." Why should there be such a built-in contrast between a theological commission and Pentecost, unless we have let our theological commissions as well as much of our church machinery function as if thought and activity were enough, forgetful that only the Holy Spirit and the experience of Him among His people are enough?

[2] *Systematic Theology*, p. 95.

things, and to lift them all up under the great, spreading canopy of God's care and concern, so that every home and business, every creation of beauty, every human relationship, every business transaction, every political decision, becomes what the Church is at its best—a sacramental channel for the Spirit of God to use. This is a vast aim. It is not asking for the moon, but it is asking for a miracle. I have the feeling that, in trying to create a nucleus of such thinking and action in the various churches, we have not only lost our aim and become involved in the problems of the institution, but that we have unintentionally ruled out of service in the New Reformation those routines and responsibilities where the ordinary person must put the major portion of time—the women in their homes, the men on their jobs. We must utterly abolish the common distinction between *religion* and *life.* We have religion in a compartment—then there is life on the other side. Religion is praying, going to church, reading the Bible. Life is raising a family, making a living, enjoying company and recreation. In a religion that began when "the Word was made flesh," such thinking is heresy. There will always be the need for spiritual beachheads, like the very best of churches, where such thinking and living may be begun and established in human lives; but these must be landings on the shores of the common life of man, and places of take-off for the invasion of the whole continent of human existence by the Spirit of God. The trouble with many spiritual awakenings is that they do not go far enough to come into real contact with so-called "secular" life.

I think that the characteristic mark of the New Reformation is going to be Spirit-filled fellowships rather than outstanding voices. God has always used personalities and will probably continue to do so always. The person that can talk to large companies of people about the necessity of coming into the stream of the Spirit, and tell them how it happens, will always be needed. But perhaps the growing, continuing awakening will consist much more in dynamic companies, where the lonely and often love-starved people of our time may experience an encircling spiritual family. Congeries of these small groups may owe their impulse and initiation to some leader; this is right and inevitable, provided the leader does not seek beyond the period of necessary training to make them "his" group. If one great voice heralds awakening anywhere (and the more, the better), the awakening must be carried forward as companies of people, mostly laymen, are taught and trained to set in motion these groups and guide them. The "word" of the Gospel is always the first step toward faith; St. Paul says, "faith cometh by hearing, and hearing by the word of God"; (Rom. 10:17) but many times this first "word" will not be the lengthy prepared address of the preacher or evangelist, but the brief, quiet-spoken, relevant word of someone who speaks out of current experience. It is the disheartening experience of many men whom God uses to set in motion true conversions, to see these people too early transferred to a church which understands little of conversion, and to see what began in fire wind up in ashes. Often clergy are too busy to give the time which newly changed people need, and sometimes they are a little suspicious of conversion anyway. What such people need is intermediate groups which become part of the real body of the new reforming movement. The Church should itself be first in realizing this and in training lay people who can lead them. We shall speak later of the manifold nature of these groups.

The New Reformation must find an experimental and experiential approach to an intellectual framework for faith. So many conventional awakenings begin with a theology that is predetermined. They speak from within a recognizable framework, acceptable to those whose conversions have hardened into viewpoints, but often anathema to those who still need to find God. The message must proceed from a sure faith in Christ in all the fullness of His claims; but in demanding the unreal and premature loyalty to Him of which we have already spoken, people are repelled and lost who might have found Him if a different approach had been used. I believe that all of us who speak for Christ today would do well to talk first about what happens to people when they find Him—not the sometimes wild and ecstatic things that go with certain conceptions, but such things as changed human relations, the discovery of new sources of power, fresh direction in life, heightened vitality, finding another way to make decisions. Sometimes this is best done by exposing them to a fellowship of experimenting people where the Holy Spirit is at work, and where the climate is the climate of events, relationships, and warmth, rather than the announcement of truth. If we begin with a true experience, found in and through persons and groups in whom the Holy Spirit is at work, we shall come in the end to a right belief. The Fundamentalistic folk want to throw the whole Book at them right away, and the very scholarly ones quickly want to "make their position clear," with the result that people's imaginations are not touched first, before someone begins moving in on their wills or asking them for the acceptance of some interpretation with their minds. Two groups need to be much less dogmatic in this area: the very conservative people who won't have anybody saved outside their own framework, and the very liberal folk who must tell you how much they don't believe! Experience first, then the interpretation of it. That seems to me good New Testament principle, and good sense.

I question whether the New Reformation will begin moralistically. Christianity, as has been said, has a moral backbone, and we must face its moral implications. But this does not come first. It is a rather advanced step to be willing to begin facing one's life in the light of Christ. I doubt if we can do it at all until some grace has been given to us. An overall recognition that we need forgiveness and redemption can come quite early in the process, and usually will—but it is more likely in our time to be redemption from meaninglessness than from mischief, from fear than from bad habits, from aimlessness than from our various addictions. Modern people easily see through the oversimplification of morality which went with an earlier kind of awakening, that if people would refrain from drinking and smoking and gambling and the usual sins of the flesh, they were "good" people. Unfortunately, some of us have met people who did none of these things, yet the love and mercy of God were not in them. Again, we have met people who sometimes slip up badly on these obvious evils, who yet were more understanding and merciful, more generous and ready to give of themselves, than some who were more pious. There is a prevalent kind of religion that seeks to dry up the wells of natural emotion and to shut them off, rather than to encourage and perhaps redirect their results in constructive ways. The people who truly belong to the New Reformation will, I think, be natural people, all the while they are also supernatural people who try to live in the Spirit. Their morality will more nearly approach St. Augustine's free but taxing rule, "Love God and do as you please." Obviously, if you truly love God you won't just do as you would please if you did not love Him; but such morality proceeds from the heart, not from petty scruple. Above all, people who belong in the New Reformation will know themselves to be forever under the one law of love, and it is a law which none can follow who is not free within from cant and pretense. If our moral convictions proceed from the love of God, they will be neither dry in their effect upon ourselves nor censorious in their effect upon other people. There are whole sections of the Christian Church that need to be redeemed from censoriousness and Pharisaism. It must be their first step toward their own New Reformation.

We must come by a larger, deeper view of conversion. I am convinced that conversion consists mainly of an initial Christian decision and of the growth which this sets in motion. Everybody needs at some time to make a Christian decision of a quite definite kind. Anyone may begin at the place where he gives as much of his life as he can to as much of Christ as he understands. The more sharp and definite this decision is, and the cleaner break it makes with the former life, the better. But the later growth will not mean unbroken progress. There will be lapses, dry times, signs of the old life reaffirming itself, in most people. Conversion is a doorway to growth, it is not a guarantee of perfection. One must bring under the total concept of conversion many steps taken toward the light, in which, be they intellectual, moral, aesthetic, or spiritual, the Holy Spirit has had a place. A part of our deepened conversion must be the willingness to accept honestly the fact of our later failures: we are such people as fail; yet we must not be disillusioned nor despairing about ourselves. Keyserling says, "He who cannot stand the tension between the inner demand to do good and the impossibility of fulfilling it, he who refuses to take up his cross—that man is truly damned." [3] There was never a time when people were more eager to find a real doorway into Christian faith and

[3] *Recovery of Truth.*

experience, and conversion is that doorway. But they must come to know that facing oneself in the light of Christ is an arduous and evolving task, lifelong in its duration. Clearness as to the challenging necessity for conversion, and modesty about how far any one person has gone in the process of it, will have to be maintained at the same time. In fact, the necessity to hold the dimension of depth, and the dimension of breadth, at the same time, is one of the clearest imperatives of the New Reformation. Only those in the Spirit—deep in Him—will be able to manage it at all.

We must ever be watching for true, fresh signs of the breaking forth of the Spirit. We shall find that much which we thought our enemy turns out to be an ally in disguise; and much that we thought to be fighting with us will be actually found fighting against us. People who hold to the Christian truth will not always be people who live in the stream of the Spirit; and we shall sometimes find those who are less dogmatic about their beliefs but live more nearly in that stream. Nels Ferré says, "Many who confess salvation are not saved, and many who think they are not may come to hear the Lord saying, 'Blessed are ye.' Charnock enunciates a great truth when he writes that 'those, therefore, are more deservedly termed atheists, who acknowledge a God, and walk as if there were none, than those (if there can be any such) that deny a God, and walk as if there were one.'"[4] The only trouble with that statement is that it finalizes the state of the nominal believer; I should prefer to draw him along, if I could, and help him to experience some of the truth he says he believes. We need him! We need also the avowed unbeliever whose life belies his starvation ration of faith. We shall need to be a little more suspicious of what passes for religious redemption, and a little more appreciative of what passes for spiritual uncertainty or even avowed unbelief, while often being found on the side of the angels. If we are ourselves living, at least at times, in the stream of the Spirit, we ought to be able to draw both these varieties of people down off their opposing banks, into the same stream with us. But it will often mean as much real change for the believer as for the unbeliever. We shall

[4] *The Christian Understanding of God,* p. 170.

find much sinfulness in the so-called saints, and much that God must approve in some of the so-called sinners. In an hour of desperation, I should far rather find myself in the hands of an alcoholic who has begun finding his way out through Alcoholics Anonymous, with as yet very little theological furniture, than of many a church member who has always behaved himself (or thinks he has), is equipped with all the theological paraphernalia, but knows little of the ingenious mercifulness of God. Coming truly into the stream will be just as much of a challenge for most people who call themselves Christians as for those who do not. We sometimes hear a conductor in a train say, at a fullstop, "Everybody change!" That will be the order of the New Reformation. Nobody can sit down with satisfaction in his own faith or virtues for five minutes, any more than he can enjoy last night's breeze on a hot summer night, or read by the electric light that shone two minutes ago in the lamp. Only the immediate presence and power of the Spirit can be the climate of the New Reformation.

The best of previous evangelical movements have been ecumenical in their aim, and not dogmatic about where their converts should find the continuation of their spiritual life and growth. There are, of course, great exceptions to this; and converts are conditioned against anything but churches which reflect exactly the outlook of the evangelist. No one can be so broad-minded as to say that all churches are of equal value, and we must help people to find a household of faith where what they have learned of God will be nourished and built up. But I am convinced our conceptions must widen. There are many Protestants that think that anyone who joins the Roman Catholic Church, or for that matter the Orthodox or the Episcopal, has strayed far from faith. And the narrowness of the Roman Catholic Church toward all other communions whatever is proverbial. We have an enormous task of education to be done. It would be well if we could persuade all evangelists to say more about the various "means of grace" to be found in various churches. It appears to me that, in the New Reformation, we shall need to make use of every kind of experience, form, and emphasis that has ever at any time been of help to anyone. It is certain that all Catholic-oriented people need to hear the evangelical message of the Gospel; it is equally certain that all Protestant-oriented people need to know more of sacramental Grace. We know now that the Reformation went too far in discarding the sacramental emphasis, and did not go far enough in emphasis upon the freedom of the Spirit as He works beyond the borders of Church or Bible. In all of this, I do not see that a churchless person has much contribution to make, as a nationless person cannot contribute much to international understanding. What is needed is a loyalty to one communion, and to one local parish of it, while at the same time one keeps the larger sympathy, knowing that the true Holy Catholic Church is found wherever the Holy Spirit is found—and He sometimes makes ducks and drakes of our little human categories and narrow concepts!

We must go farther still. I believe that, while the Christian Church must be the initiator of the New Reformation, and that we shall get the most help from those portions of it that are truly Evangelical, it should and will go far beyond the confines of the Christian Church. The Holy Spirit surely is found in some measure in every religion, and we must make common cause with Him there. When we say of Him, in the Creed, "Who spake by the prophets," we certainly mean the Hebrew prophets who were before Christ. But is He confined to them? What about Mohammedan prophets, Hindu prophets, Buddhist prophets? And what of scientific prophets, and economic prophets, and educational prophets, and philosophical prophets? All truth is His truth, and He is the Lord of it. Does He not wish all that He has created to be used in this vast all-out effort which the New Reformation should be? One hears of a resurgence of some of the ancient Eastern faiths. I think we should rejoice in it. Blank unbelief is not such good soil for Christian sowing as loyalty to what truth one knows. In many places here at home, one witnesses a great revival of Judaism. Near my home in Maryland, where I am writing, there have been erected a remarkable number of new synagogues and schools. Is not this a better sign in God's ancient people than the exclusively mercantile pursuits with which their names are so frequently associated? It must be the hope of all Christians that any experience of God's Spirit will eventually lead to faith in Christ. But I firmly believe that this will more likely take place through another faith than in a vacuum. I find myself completely at variance with the view sometimes found among Roman Catholics, that it is better to be nothing than to be Protestant; and among Protestants, that it is better to belong nowhere than to Rome. I think it is far better to be a good Jew, or a good Mohammedan, or a good Buddhist, than to be nothing at all. It is going to take all of us working together under the Holy Spirit to swell the tide of such a movement as we need. In some instances anything like outward co-operation will be impossible; this is why we need the overall generalship of the Holy Spirit, who has His own secret avenues to many whom we cannot influence. And it is why we need hundreds of thousands of converted and convinced Christians who will, by their appreciation and courtesy, commend Christ to others. We must always remember that, while almost all men will covertly or openly agree that God has never so resided in any other as He did in Christ, we who call ourselves by His Name have often done Him singular despite and disservice, and signally failed to live sufficiently in His Spirit. Our certainty about Him may be witnessed best through great uncertainty about ourselves as His servants. Those of other faiths often see and remark this; let us meet their strictures with honest confession and admission, rather than with any argument that would defend ourselves. In this area, most of us are without defense.

We who live in countries that still enjoy freedom are little cognizant of the struggle that won and kept freedom in the past, and need occasional reminding of Luther's words: "You ought to beware of thinking that Christ will achieve things in the earth quietly and softly, when you see that He fought with His own blood, and afterward all the martyrs." [5] Free men can enjoy their liberties with little awareness of the investment in faith and sacrifice that has gone into them. The forces of darkness rage today, and their magnitude is unimaginable to any of us that have not suffered directly from them in personal ways. If the course of any New Reformation were as moderate and considerate as what we have been suggesting here, without the iron of complete dedication and determination to reinforce it, the

[5] Quoted in Harry Emerson Fosdick, ed., *Great Voices of the Reformation*, p 70.

dark forces could and would laugh it out of countenance. What we are suggesting in no way smacks of weakness: it is merely as strainless and unfanatical a kind of strength as we can discover. But I have always noticed that the one profoundest weakness of all totalitarian systems and the people who advocate them is their want of humor, especially about themselves and their heavy-footed movements. It could be that there is a force in the world greater than armies, and greater than diplomacy—the spiritual force of God which finds no place for fanatical self-assertion, takes its faith and cause seriously, but never itself; and which might in the end be the thing that will laugh dictatorships out of countenance.

I do not know a better Credo for the New Reformation than that which is suggested in a letter from a lay friend of mine, Roger C. Tredwell. He says, "I don't think we need another Pentecost. It is here for all time. The Holy Spirit was not meant, I think, to be given only to the disciples. He is here now, forevermore revealing the Living Christ. The Father's greatest gift to mankind was the Son, and the Son's greatest gift was the Holy Spirit. What I think we need to do and what the Church needs to do is to open our hearts and minds that the Holy Spirit may be allowed to do His mighty works within us."

6

The Holy Spirit and Evangelism

To be in the stream of the Holy Spirit, and to wish to draw others into that same stream, are not two things, but two sides of one thing. One who has found a real answer can hardly keep quiet about it, especially when he sees another in the same confusion which was his. The sharing of it comes later than the finding of it, but no one really experiences what Christ gave to the world without wanting other people to experience this same Power. The Church, therefore, is not charged with evangelism as one of its responsibilities; there *is* no Church where evangelism is not living and current. Dr. Emil Brunner says "the Church exists by mission as fire exists by burning."[1] You cannot separate between the fire and the burning, and you cannot separate between the Church and the impartation of its own message to others. Alcoholics Anonymous has learned this much better than great segments of the Church itself, and declares, in Tradition 5, "Each group has but one primary purpose —to carry its message to the alcoholics who still suffer."

We must go back to our foundation and our commission, and see what the Holy Spirit's place is in all this. Jesus said, " 'If any man is thirsty, he can come to me and drink! The man who believes in me, as the Scripture said, will have rivers of living water flowing from his inmost heart.' Here he was speaking

[1] Quoted by Simeon Stylites in *The Christian Century,* Aug. 11, 1954.

about the Holy Spirit which those who believe in him would receive" (St. John 7:37-39, Phillips). He tells us that He is the satisfaction of human need; and that when He meets that human need, the recipient of His help will inevitably be a channel of power which the Holy Spirit will give to him.

True evangelism has to do with helping people into Christian faith and life. It is one thing to call for an increase in the birth rate, or to think of what a lovely thing is the life of a baby, and quite another thing to know the struggle and pain some mothers undergo in childbirth. There must be a follow-up of evangelism, as there must be care and feeding for the newborn child; but the first thing is to get him here. This is the job of the obstetrician, not the pediatrician. The evangelist is primarily an obstetrician. He is concerned with birth, "new birth." The heart and core of that new birth is a Christian decision. The well-known report of the Archbishops' Commission in England, called "Toward the Conversion of England," explains, "In all evangelism there is the duty of working for a decision of the will. Evangelists, therefore, should take warning that it is incumbent upon them to act under the conscious guidance of the Holy Spirit, and in accordance with that respect for personality which was so marked a feature of our Lord's dealing with individuals." [2] And Dr. Paul Tillich's idea is, "True communication of the Gospel means making possible a definite decision for or against it." He calls the Gospel "a matter of decision."

This decision requires content. It is a decision of the whole personality, not of the mind or the heart or the will acting unilaterally, but all of them in concert. One uses his head to assess the world and life and his life, and to understand what he can of Christ. One uses his heart because "out of it are the issues of life," it is thought of as the seat of human emotion, and human emotion it is which usually causes things to happen in human personalities. One uses the will, because, as Dr. Brunner writes, "will is the material factor of faith." [3] It takes a motion of the will to set the process of faith going. This new, emerging factor of faith seems to gather its momentum from deep within the personality, called forth by something or someone outside to

[2] P. 68.
[3] *Pastoral Psychology,* June 1956, p. 10.

which faith "goes out" and to which it attaches itself. According to Unamuno, ". . . faith is an act of the will—it is a movement of the soul towards a practical truth, towards a person, towards something that makes us not merely comprehend life, but makes us live."[4] We let faith happen, or we prevent it from happening, according to a deep willingness or unwillingness within us. It is not that faith is mere wishful thinking, but that it cannot become living power without our consent. And the best provoker of it is probably an appeal to the imagination first, rather than to thought, feeling, or decision. Imagination dwells on the great thing called faith, which some have found and have, and which sets up a longing within us. When the Spirit of God, which we believe prompted this whole process from the start, sees this tiny flame of faith, He blows upon it and feeds it till it bursts into an inner fire.

D. T. Niles, of India, states that "evangelism is one beggar telling another where to get bread." None of us can ever body forth the Gospel completely, nor "be" it for another, except in a most limited sense: only Jesus ever "was" what He taught. The rest of us can only say, "There it is!" and point to it. We can be God's "doormen," whose work it is to let people in. Some may call this a menial and temporary task, but—let us face it—until it has been accomplished no living, no hospitality, and no human relations within the house are possible. Some of us need to be specially watchful of the beginnings, and signs of beginnings, of the life in the Spirit.

If we are to become increasingly proficient in this work (and what can be of greater importance?), then we must learn something of the *trackage* of Christian experience, the "way," the psychology, the technique, if you like, by which people come into contact with the Spirit of God and begin the new life in Him and grow in it. We must know the "cluster of active ingredients," as Melvin Evans calls them. The average Christian has some slight idea of the content of his religion, but almost no idea of the process by which it takes its beginning and develops in the life of an individual. He has heard the content many times, but he has never been where he might see the process

[4] *The Tragic Sense of Life*, p. 191.

taking place before his eyes, as it is seen in an open meeting of Alcoholics Anonymous, for instance. Someone said that evangelism is to religion what salesmanship is to business. Do not scorn the commercial parallel: rather let yourself be stung by the aptness, and ask yourself how many "sales" you have ever made? Is there anyone that is fundamentally different because of your life and witness? There should be. We are meant to be pipes, not buckets! Some Christians are close to God but remote from people. Some are close to people, but remote from God. Some are close to neither: and some are close to both. Of these last come the real "fishers of men."

At its best, evangelism is part of living. It is not a special activity. Its setting is not in the dim light of a church, nor the professional climate of an office or study; its setting is in the very midst of life. We must always remember St. Paul's great twofold order, "first that which is natural, and afterward that which is spiritual" (I. Cor. 15:46). We must know people, like them, enjoy them, make friends with them, take trouble for them, before it may ever be right to "speak" to them about spiritual matters. It is not that we ever earn the right to do this, so much as that we wait for a relation to them in which it becomes the almost inevitable next step, if we have built solidly in the relationship itself.

Let me give two examples.

Not long ago I heard a young woman tell about having had a great experience of Christ herself: she was radiant with it, excited about it, and wanted to tell the members of her bridge club about it. She realized she could not ask those in the group to pray, it would shock and lose them. She did suggest to one of them that she read a certain book, but this sent her off into another direction. It happened, however, that this woman, who had been put off by the suggestion about the book, was just then furnishing a new house, and her mind was on drapes and coverings for her furniture. So my friend began to enter into that situation with her, and said, "Why don't you bring the samples you are considering to the club next week, and let us talk them over with you—we'd be so interested." This she did; and having got into her emotions through her real interests, it was not long before they were talking about somebody they both knew who was in great need. And when toward the end of this session she gently suggested they might all pray for this woman, everyone was happy to do it, including the lady with the samples. Later she got them all into a steadily functioning group! Now some people are so busy getting a human contact that they spend years doing it, and as a result get lost in the samples. But the wise person begins with something of present, common interest, and builds on the relationship that is thus established.

I know a young couple who are missionaries in an Oriental country. Before they were married, she was a model, and a remarkably beautiful girl. Not long ago he wrote me, "K—— is teaching a course on 'charm' for the summer activities of the army and civilians here. We really enjoyed planning together this course, and how she might get across that inward beauty is more important than outward." They know enough to begin where people are, and to build on their present interest, and to make faith relevant for that interest. Some of the very pious of certain modern schools of theological thought will tell you this runs a perilous risk of "using" God. Yes, I suspect it does; and I suspect that nearly all religion that seeks from God the answer to our needs is of exactly the same nature, including that of the proponents of this particular school of thought. We were all children once, and sometimes shamelessly "used" our parents. They did not disown us for this, but sought gradually to teach us some semblance of unselfishness towards them. So, I believe, does God.

There is a reason, I suspect, why we love St. Luke's Gospel as the most "human" of them all in its picture of Jesus. Someone said that St. Matthew shows us all the mountaintops; and St. Luke takes us to one dinner party after another!

The place where great numbers of people first seek contact with the stream of the Spirit is in church. The climate and atmosphere may be what consciously or unconsciously attracts or repels them. But ever so much depends upon the preaching. Do not far too many of us preachers deal with some fragment of the great Truth of the Gospel, and should we not go far more often for its great central reality? This must always be the confrontation of individual souls with Jesus Christ, even if this confrontation is begun by introducing them to the stream of the

Spirit. It will not be done so much by saying the right words, nor by any special clarity of description: it will be evident to them that we know the stream of the Spirit ourselves, even though they know we do not always live in it. When a sermon becomes an essay instead of a witness from or about someone who knows the stream of the Spirit, the power has departed. Yes, we shall need to give them intellectual help; and they will need comfort and strength, too. But too often we are preaching to somebody who is not present—the homiletics professor at the seminary, or some of our classmates there whose regard and agreement we crave—rather than to the hungry people right in front of us. Never mind what the theological professors, or our theological peers, think of us: let us fit our talks to the people before us.

Most sermons are footnotes to the Gospel, which would be helpful if we knew the rest of it; but when we do not, these talks are sometimes positive deterrents from the Gospel, deflectors toward side issues. I think that our general statements and generalizations must give way to much more presentation of personal stories about modern people, delineating their struggles, showing how faith became real, and then what it is doing for them as they seek to live and work in the stream. Preaching ought to be a fair cross-section of a minister's current life—not blatant autobiography, of course, but full of such material as makes it plain he knows the stream of the Spirit. Much of our Lord's preaching undoubtedly arose out of situations He created by acting, then the people reacted, then He gave His word. I think He did not expect to do as much by words as we do: words only interpreted and threw light on the power that had already been manifested. We should preach more simply, and much better, if we lived more amidst His miracles today. There is a vivid testimony to the strength of words spoken in the presence of spiritual power, in Acts 8:6-8, where we read, "And the multitudes with one accord gave heed to what was said by Philip, when they heard him and saw the signs which he did. For unclean spirits came out of many who were possessed, crying with a loud voice; and many who were paralyzed or lame were healed. So there was much joy in that city" (RSV). What a picture of the stream—and of the preaching that should characterize us if we lived more consistently in it!

This brings up another most important point about evangelism. It concerns our use of simple words and language. Whether in the preaching and witnessing of the clergy, or the speaking and witnessing of lay people, we must err rather on the side of what is sometimes called, in a good phrase, "the vulgar tongue." Jesus spoke in that tongue. C. S. Lewis says of Him, "He preaches, but He does not lecture. He uses paradox, proverb, exaggeration, parable, irony; even (I mean no irreverence) the 'wisecrack.'" [5] Nobody ever said he could not understand Him. There is much intellectual snobbishness in some men's preaching. Martin Luther spoke differently. Erik Erikson says of him, "His style indicates his conviction that a thing said less elegantly and meant more truly is better work, and better craftsmanship in communication." [6]

Hear part of a letter from a layman who has been at this business for a good many years. He is speaking of the way we fall into a religious "jargon." He writes, "The more I think about it, the more I am forced to the conclusion that this fault does not exist solely with parsons—it's a failing of almost anybody who has spent years in any profession. When we train new men in the advertising business, we have to watch carefully this tendency to assume people know something they don't know. When a subject is very familiar to you and you talk of it with abandon, you are most apt to talk from the point where you stand, instead of trying to get to the level of your audience . . . I believe with all my heart that a man who opens his heart and mind to God will be guided. God will take him right where he is and show him the way. And yet when I talk like this to some people I must be very careful because I find again and again they haven't the foggiest idea what I'm talking about. However, I find that if I go back to my original days, I begin to make some sense for them. I found that in talking with my sons, I got much further when I went back to what I was doing ten, fifteen, twenty or twenty-five years ago."

After a very heavy theological presentation at the Evanston

[5] *Reflections on the Psalms,* pp. 112-13.
[6] *Young Man Luther,* Erik H. Erikson, p. 220.

Assembly of the World Council of Churches, the late Bishop Berggrav of Oslo was heard to remark in an aside, "The word became theology and did *not* dwell among us." Let us all be warned. People need, and want, genuine theology which is like the bony structure of the body—necessary, but a lot more welcome when covered with healthy flesh. In our preaching, as in our whole conduct of the life and work of the Church, we are long on truth and short on experience. We fill people till they are stuffed with Christian ideas, but these are not often enough manifested by Christian events. We have an Incarnational *theology* in our Christian faith. We need also an Incarnational *psychology* in the presentation of it. Dave Garroway once interviewed H. V. Kaltenborn about Hitler's power to sway and influence people. Kaltenborn said Hitler followed three rules: Make it simple—Say it often—Make it burn. It is a good succinct course in preaching!

Who needs to be evangelized? Is it the heathen abroad? What about the heathen at home? Are all the heathen outside of the Church? The black-and-white division between believers and unbelievers leads to some strange conclusions. I am appalled at the ease with which certain evangelicals consign millions of people to hell forever. One of them was talking about this to me one day, apparently with a quite easy mind about it. I said, "My friend, let's look at this thing squarely. These unbelieving people in India, Africa, China, the islands of the sea, have not heard the message of the Gospel, and cannot fairly be judged about what they do not know. But you KNOW that they have never heard the Gospel; and you sit home in a comfortable church, making a comfortable living. It seems to me if anybody is going to fry in hell, it's going to be the folk who know but do not care." A student is said to have once asked Dr. Spurgeon whether he thought the heathen who had never heard the Gospel would be saved, and Dr. Spurgeon said, "It is more of a question with me whether we, who have the Gospel, and fail to give it to those who do not have it, can be saved."

Now and then you read a derogatory report about the results of an evangelistic effort somewhere, which complains that so many converts were already members of the Church! As if church membership guaranteed spiritual power, convertedness, or even any knowledge of living in the stream of the Spirit! Who needs conversion more than some of our prominent churchfolk, desperately busy about the little affairs of local parish life, gossipy, meddlesome, ineffective? If these people, and some of us their ministers, had a little more of the love of God in us, matters would be very different for the Church as a whole. Evangelism is not to make church members: evangelism is to make Christians—maybe out of church members along with the rest. Let us be done with the hue and cry that so many converts already belong to the Church. We need it as much as anybody on the outside.

What qualities are needed if one seeks to do this kind of work? We are not primarily thinking of large-scale evangelism which is beyond the scope of most of us, but of man-to-man work which is within our reach. We must ourselves have made a genuine spiritual start, given as much of ourselves as we can to as much of Christ as we understand, or else we have nothing to say. This does not mean either perfection or great spiritual maturity; and we shall find that we ourselves learn and grow as we seek to give away what Christ has given to us. We ought to be praying as often as we can think of it: for it is prayer primarily that keeps us in the stream of the Spirit. Ordinarily we need to feel some sense of God's guidance relative to another person we seek to win—that this person is our job, that this is the time, or this the way to begin. My friend in the steel mill in Pittsburgh, David Griffith, says, "You've got to love them, you've got to be with them, you've got to pray for them, you've got to spend time with them." J. B. Phillips says, ". . . people can only be LOVED into the Kingdom of God." [7]

But what qualities should characterize us if we are to be effective with ordinary modern people? Let me give six of them.

The first is good manners. Only people who have "gentle" feelings themselves can be sensitive to those of others; and without sensitivity, both to the motions of the Spirit and to the moods of people, we shall bungle this work. The abrupt intrusion of religion without natural preliminary, the failure to exercise courtesy at all times, can spoil an opportunity. Most people

[7] *New Testament Christianity*, p. 76.

are eager to impart something personal of themselves, and welcome it if you impart something of yourself: but not if it all comes out at once. If they know of your interest in religion already sometimes you will better win them with a little restraint, which is not inconsistent with enthusiasm and eagerness. This kind of gentlemanliness is a refinement which faith in Christ gives to human beings. You won't necessarily have it because you went to a fine school, or were brought up among privileged people: some of these are crude and bad-mannered. To be personal a moment, I do not know many people who better define the word "gentleman" than Ralston Young, Red Cap 42 at Grand Central Station in New York, and very few who are such effective witnesses for Christ. At ease with people, always putting them at ease, he seems always to *say* the right thing because he is *feeling* the right thing. This is not just the pat or the polite thing, this is the word that warms and draws people, that understands them and draws them out on spiritual things. I suppose that the reason why sinners were always so much at home with Christ was that He was always so courteous to them—though this does not always apply in the case of the Pharisees: and sometimes with them we, too, may need to say very blunt words.

The second quality I would dare to call a good worldly sense. The Gospel builds a bridge between God and man, and a bridge must be solid on both ends. We must know human nature—its lovableness, its deviousness, its nobility, its contemptibleness. Sentimentality, naïveté, innocence, such as we associate with certain kinds of "religious" people, will be a hindrance. It is the false saint who is simpering: the real ones are usually shrewd and realistic. If God so loved the world that He sent His Son, we ought to love it, too—not in what is usually called a "worldly" sense, but as sharing in the joys and sadnesses and realities of its life, not as pious spectators on the sidelines. Within, we ought to be deeply cut away from the world: but outwardly we ought to be more identified with it than anyone else. Our Lord was. He belonged to both worlds, and so must we. We must have a real love for those things and those people that, when loved too much, or loved the wrong way, make us undesirably worldly. Christ established a foothold within this world before He set out to change it. We must do the same.

A third factor in good fishers of men is humor. I do not mean only the ability to tell a good story, though this is not to be minimized: I mean really the kind of understanding that we are ourselves part of the problem even when we talk about the cure, that we know we do not have all the answers, that we do not take ourselves seriously. The danger with people who have got far enough to witness is that they become self-righteous or pontifical. Humor soon scatters these postures. A good laugh, even a very healthy smile, brings us back to earth, deflates whatever gathers in us of the "stuffed shirt." Humor often forms a new level of reality between people. Some people have an idea that humor and religion are strangers. We can laugh until we mention God: then we must go solemn. This is sheer heresy! There are tens of thousands of Christians who need to hear this, for by their solemnity they drive away the very people they say they want to reach. It must be consecrated humor, else it will not be a channel for the Spirit. But nothing else reveals more of our understanding of God, life, and people than the power to laugh—especially at ourselves. The whole spiritual adventure should be exciting, studded with awkward moments now and then because of our frailties, yet over-all full of a kind of understanding which often best manifests itself to others in humor.

Fourth, I would mention humility. This does not mean the self-conscious cowardice which fears to step up to the bat, and begs off from this work because of immaturity or inexperience: that is not humility, it is usually pride backfiring—we fear to fail, to appear foolish. Humility, moreover, may not be without confidence in what one has the power to do. It would not be humility for Marian Anderson to say she could not sing: it would be plain untruth. Humility is not inconsistent with doing one's best—that is why the order to the novice, in *The Nun's Story,* to fail in her examinations in order to cultivate humility, was so deeply immoral. But for Marian Anderson to feel that her voice is God-given, and to use it for His glory—that is real humility. Humility has to do, I think, not so much with one's emotions about an immediate performance—a song, a sermon, a piece of writing, a business sale—as about whether one feels that God is the center of creation and life, the Giver of all one's talents. The best offset to human pride is always gratefulness. It is better to seek gratefulness than humility; for real gratitude will bring humility with it.

Fifth, we need honesty. At some point in the conversation, or series of conversations, there will be the time to be honest about our own experience and the Christ who caused it. If we come at this too soon, we will lose people. If we begin with this, before they have had time to recognize our manners, knowledge of life, fun, and simplicity, we shall make them uncomfortable. As we are with them, and there is an exchange of experiences, we will get into general talk about life and its problems; as we move on to some of our own, about which we talk naturally, letting them see how close to life faith comes, they will go with us. The response is almost automatic. It is not necessary for our problem to be identically the same as theirs; the honest expression of some need in our own life and what Christ is doing to help us solve it will often provide the occasion for honesty both ways, and this is an atmosphere in which God can work. This honesty does not mean accusation of the other person if we know something against him—far better where possible to create such an atmosphere as causes him to want to be honest, and let him tell this himself, than to throw the problem at him in judgment. The first, best honesty concerns our own faults and sins, and what we are beginning to find in Christ.

The sixth quality I would name is joy. This is inseparable from a full Christian life. It is the first thing people see in us, or miss in us. Some are only joyous, outwardly, when they can forget their religion and have a good time; they have never gone far enough to know the joy of wholehearted discipleship. The true joy lies in loving and serving Christ. If we have it, we can't hide it: if we haven't got it, we can't fake it. Ralston Young says of the old colored woman in his apartment house who first turned him to think of spiritual things, "She had the gaiety. She was a live wire. Buoyancy, that's what I mean—its bubblin'—never a dull day!" Joy marks the indisputable Presence of the Holy Spirit in us. It is akin to enthusiasm. It is the "outsides" of faith. This joy is aware of God, of His working and presence, and of the coincidences that go along with real faith. It is not dependent on an exuberant temperament, nor favoring circumstances: one has seen it in people under great trial and duress, even in pain and suffering. Not long ago, reading J. B. Phillips' translation of the New Testament, I came to the place where Jesus is talking about John the Baptist's asceticism, and then of His own more natural approach to life. Jesus says this of Himself, "The Son of Man came, enjoying life, and you say, 'Look, a drunkard and a glutton, a bosom friend of the tax-collector and the outsider!'" What a picture of Him, "enjoying life," a "bosom-friend of outsiders!" Is it not wonderful to remember that He who out of all the world was closest to God, was also closest to men; and that He who was unmistakably a "Man of sorrows" was also such a "Man of joy"? "Enjoying life"—when have we heard of this as a badge of authenticity for those who would be used of God to bring people to God? Well, it has the best accreditation in the world: it comes from Jesus Christ Himself.

There is no pattern for an effective witness. But I suggest that these steps and headings may be well to remember:

1. Imagination.
2. Need.
3. Sharing.
4. Decision.
5. Prayer.
6. Fellowship.
7. Witness.

All of this which we have been saying concerns the inculcation of personal religious experience and faith. This is and will always be foundational in the Christian scheme of things. Unless some wider spirit, more favorable to reason, more congenial to modern minds, is found, the ways of an older evangelism will fail with many today. But when certain scholars and enthusiasts for the social application of the Gospel complain that there is not enough of this kind of relevance in simple presentations of the Christian Gospel, such for instance as Billy Graham's, I should like to take issue with them. I think they forget how many people, in the churches as well as outside them, have never yet had a decisive experience of Christ, and this must always be an intensely personal thing. Still more do I want to say to them that, for Graham to talk more than he already does about such a thing as the race question, or other social issues, would be to put the cart before the horse. I remember reading with great appreciation some years ago J. W. Bready's, *England Before and After Wesley.* The great social reforms that stemmed from the Wesleyan revival came *after* the first spiritual impact, some of them long after. In his book on *Revivalism and Social Reform,* Dr. Timothy L. Smith says, ". . . in the nineteenth century revival measures, being new, usually went hand in hand with progressive theology and humanitarian concern . . . the evangelists played a key role in the widespread attack upon slavery, poverty and greed. They thus helped prepare the way both in theory and in practise for what later became known as the social gospel." [8] He points out their effect in greater tolerance and interdenominational co-operation, and their result and fruit in what is usually called the "social gospel." I would strongly suspect that one reason why the Methodists eventually had such a profound sociological effect was that they first did a magnificent job of getting people personally changed. If some of the modern evangelists have been scant in their emphasis on social fruits, it may also be said that many of the social-gospel folk have also been scant in providing a decisive and life-transforming personal experience of Christ. It is not a matter of "either . . . or": it is a matter of "both . . . and." But, as education is a matter of primary teaching, and of university teaching, they cannot both be given at the same time. The same men who accuse personal-religion enthusiasts of expecting too many "sudden" conversions must not themselves expect to give people the whole of the Gospel at once, nor look for effects now which can only come about when personal foundations have been laid.

I cannot but quote a paragraph from *Christianity Today,*[9] by the editor. He writes, "Criticize Mr. Graham as men may for halting short of a complete agenda for civilization, his message rings with the only priorities discoverable in the Acts of the Apostles: the death of Jesus Christ for sinners, his resurrection and exaltation as Lord and Savior, and the indispensability of man's total commitment to the living God. In an age wherein social gospelism had come to disparage if not to disdain evangelism, Graham's plea for decision drew phenomenal response in

[8] Pp. 60, 8. See also pp. 84-92.
[9] March 30, 1959.

New York, San Francisco, London, Glasgow, Berlin, Madras and Melbourne that perplexed earnest churchmen who sought to improve Christianity's position mainly by unifying its organizational structures." If there are those who think that any kind of evangelism whatever errs on the side of being too personal, let us face in all frankness the failure of our intellectually and socially oriented brands of Christianity to be personal enough. Evangelism is primarily concerned with helping people find and take those spiritual first steps that lead into Christian faith and experience. Its social effects cannot be expected to follow at once, any more than a newborn child can be expected to walk at once. He will walk, he is intended to walk, and if he does not try to walk within reasonable time he is a sick child. But not the day after he was born! Let us allow for growth, for the growingly concrete promptings of the Holy Spirit. When I hear some men failing to give thanks for spiritual fruits such as God gives to Billy Graham, but instead charting the exact path along which the Holy Spirit is expected to lead them at once, I think they come very near to the blasphemy of playing God themselves. In the day of a new kind of evangelism, which we need, let us give thanks and be appreciative of *all* the fruits of the Spirit which we see, whether or not they happen to be congenial to us.

The spirit of evangelism is most important. It must be ecumenical in its very nature—evangelism which merely steals people from one church or denomination and enrolls them in another is a doubtful activity for a Christian. We need to be convinced, yet humble—persuasive, yet tolerant—persistent, yet natural. If it were not for the mixture of the Holy Spirit's guidance and power with our own efforts, they would come to little.

The churches and their leaders make many fine pronouncements about evangelism. Sometimes they seem more in love with their well-pondered and highly polished words than with anything actually done and accomplished in this area. Drawing up ideal pictures of evangelism is not necessarily evangelism, and may take their minds in such theoretical directions that nothing actual (and therefore limited and imperfect) does anything but draw criticisms. It is much easier to get some fine minds together and draw up a declaration of "what we need" than to get some warmhearted and human people together that will start something in a store or an office. It has become correct now in my particular Communion to talk about evangelism: but sometimes I wonder whether what we *call* evangelism is evangelism at all, or rather a special brand of minor excitement and low-grade spiritual virus which does not offend our Anglican sensibilities. Bishop Burrill, of Chicago, says that "evangelism in the Episcopal Church is being sacrificed to the needs of the program and the schedule of worship." No words could be more true.

Let us ponder this comment from Dr. George Sweazey: [10] "The Church must jealously guard this word 'evangelism.' It can be stolen, not only by those who would limit it to what is too narrow, but by those who would waste it on what is too broad. The task of reaching outside the Church to bring people to faith in Christ and membership in His Church is a distinct and specific duty. The word 'evangelism' is the word that has been traditionally used for this purpose. When the word is obscured, the duty is obscured."

The grace, the power, the "urge" to evangelism is not within ourselves. It is the gift of the Holy Spirit Himself. Dr. Hendrik Kraemer says, "The Holy Spirit is the Baptizer of the Church into witness-bearing." [11]

[10] Quoted in *Christianity Today,* June 22, 1959, p. 22.
[11] *A Theology of the Laity,* p. 132.

7

The Holy Spirit and the Church

If the great gift of Christ to His people, when He was physically withdrawn from them, was the Holy Spirit, why do we need the Church at all? This has been a tantalizing question and preoccupation for many, and they have sought to create a free and unorganized fellowship, only to find in the end that human things *must* use concrete means to survive and progress at all. We need the Church because there is a definitive Christian faith which people have to know, and on the truths of which they are intended to feed. We need the Church because each of us individually should have the corrective and the inspiration of other believers, including those of the past. We need the Church because common worship is something besides an aggregate of individual prayer: it is a necessary corporate act. We need the Church because Christ offered to His people, in Baptism and Holy Communion, means of sacramental grace which only the Church is authorized to dispense. We need the Church because no one of us is individually strong enough to stand up to the evil that is in the world and in himself. We need the Church because Christ obviously created it to be the spearhead of His Kingdom on earth. Spiritual realities just do not continue in this world without some kind of body—as human beings do not.

It is always the hope and usually the intention of the pioneers in a spiritual movement that *this* movement will never slip down to the level of routine and organization. Yet, no matter how powerful at the beginning, we know of no spiritual movement in Christian history that has not experienced a "hardening of the arteries" with age. It was true even of the movement following Pentecost. Dr. Van Dusen calls this "the logic of spiritual vitality," and says we have seen it "re-enacted again and again in the pilgrimage of the Christian Church, whereby a period of intense and creative religious renewal is unfailingly succeeded by an aftermath of gradually diminishing spiritual vigor but increasing theological and organizational rigidity, then by a time of comparative sterility—until revival bursts forth afresh, and the curve of descending life and power is re-enacted." [1] He gives later in his book a summary of "the fate of the Holy Spirit at the hands of the theologians and Church officials across the centuries," and calls it "on the whole, a pathetic and tragic story." [2] These are the historical steps and stages:

The indubitable centrality of the Holy Spirit in the life and message of the Earliest Church.

Its regnancy in the faith and thought of the Apostle Paul.

Its capture and imprisonment by Catholic ecclesiasticism.

Its release and renewal in every epoch of spiritual revival.

Its reimprisonment by the classic Reformers within the text of Scripture.

Its emancipation with power by the so-called "Radical Reformation," the "Reformation Sects."

Its gradual quiescence into innocuous conventionality in their later respectability.

Today, its reappearance in familiar excess and wonted power in the contemporary "sects."

He explains something of why this happens, saying, ". . . the Holy Spirit has always been troublesome, disturbing because it has seemed to be unruly, radical, unpredictable. It is always embarrassing to ecclesiasticism and baffling to ethically-grounded, responsible, durable Christian devotion. And so it has been carefully taken in hand by Church authorities, whether Catholic or Protestant, and securely tethered in impotence . . . professional

[1] *Op. cit.*, p. 27.
[2] *Ibid.*, p. 125.

ecclesiasts constitutionally distrust the novel, the unconventional and, even more, the reproachful and the challenging. The corrective of internal purification seems to them too precarious and too gentle; they incline toward the sterner surety of external control. They may seek to discredit and disown what they distrust . . . or they may accomplish the same end by taking the troublesome disturber under their patronage and emasculating it through redefinition and regulation."[3] It is not difficult to discern, beneath this scholarly review, the writer's own passionate disapproval of what these "theologians and Church officials" have done and still do.

To offer anything like a solution to this age-old and never-solved problem would be to assume omniscience. And yet it would seem incumbent upon any dedicated Christian to be concerned about this cycle, to be watchful and distrustful when Catholic folk try to ground and domesticate the Holy Spirit in an ecclesiastical organization and authority, or when Protestant folk equally err by seeking to confine Him to the written Word of the past. We must at least seek to lengthen the time of inspiration, and to shorten that of sterility. Trained and experienced leaders must not be infected with the skepticism which, mindful of dry times to come, belittles the "times of refreshing" (Acts 3:19), nor be afraid to face their often humble origin, unpredictable duration, or surprising historical turns. Nor must those who experience the glorious warmth and reality of the awakening time fear to recognize that it will not always be so. We should be ill content with the roots of flowers which never bear blooms, or with fruit trees that never have apples or pears on them. But the life of the plant and the tree goes on through cold winter months, while the flowers and fruits occur for a relatively brief season in summer and fall. What the Church must look out for is plants that never bloom, and trees that never bear fruit. We must face the fact that there are thousands of churches and ministers and devoted lay people who have never seen anything remotely like Pentecost or its lineal descendants.

Dr. Hendrik Kraemer says that ". . . we have got into the habit of not (as the Bible insists) considering Renewal the

[3] *Ibid.*, pp. 126, 79.

perennial and constant rule for the Church, but regard it as a miraculous episode which befalls us from time to time." [4]

So the first thing the Church must do (and it applies to us all, whether or not we think we understand spiritual awakenings and contribute to them) is to admit that our financial and organizational and building operations have far outrun our spiritual aims and achievements. Our "successes" are often dubious. Are we saying and doing things that deeply heal, help, change, release people? Or are we running ecclesiastical business organizations as large, as efficient, as prosperous, as we can make them? Says Dr. Tillich, "The first word . . . to be spoken by religion to the people of our time must be a word spoken against religion." [5] I am a little weary of people who have their ax out for the Church in merely negative ways; but I think we must face our failures and shortcomings.

Let me present four pictures of life in the Church.

The Archbishop of Canterbury says that he found a large number of choirboys among the prisoners in a prison which he visited. He said he could point to no moral. I hope it is not presumptuous of me to think I see a very plain moral: the life of the parish churches where these boys had sung simply did not have anything vital enough to capture their imaginations or get them changed. It was taken for granted that a choirboy was a "good" boy, and a good boy does not need any spiritual conversion.

Not long ago I heard a clergyman in quite a large church say that he spent every Tuesday afternoon, all of it, untangling the problems of his staff; and that by the time evening came, he was a whipped man. One is glad to hear of a minister giving time to his own staff: but one whole afternoon of every week "untangling their problems"? What does this suggest of a spiritual level? Where is the Holy Spirit, with His power to guide and to unify?

A minister writes me, "I have just returned from our Provincial meeting—a thoroughly feckless affair, lacking in any semblance of ecclesiastical statesmanship, no vision, no daring, no enthusiasm, no awareness at all, apparently, of the state the

[4] *A Theology of the Laity*, p. 86.
[5] *The Protestant Era*, p. 185.

world is in." Are our clergy gatherings and official church meetings really beyond the immediate touch of the Holy Spirit, because of a tight, unbreakable schedule, because of anything like manifest spiritual power being irrelevant, because saying a formal prayer at the beginning is nod enough to God?

A college undergraduate was taken to an official national gathering of laymen to speak about what was happening in conversions and small groups on his campus. He and several others with him, talking along the same line, spoke well. But it was an early afternoon hour. The delegates slumped in chairs and on sofas while these very electric men talked of what was happening spiritually on the campus and in their businesses. The delegates seemed not to know what was being talked about, for none of the speakers said anything about a committee or a budget. The college undergraduate was seriously considering the ministry. But going back on the train he remarked, "If that is the Church, to hell with it!" He never went into the ministry. I had the feeling that these older men, so set on laymen's organization, so little understanding of how laymen can make a real spiritual attack on an actual situation, threw a bucket of cold water on his aspirations. These were avowedly Christian men; but they were so busy doing the Church's business the wrong way that they completely failed one highly potential young man.

Unhappily these instances are far too typical to make us comfortable. We get bogged down with the necessary organizational arrangements of the Church, and almost before we know it, these are taking the major part of our time, our best efforts, our creative concern. I think of a deeply converted and profoundly changed man who went into the ministry with the highest hopes and intentions; but five years later told me he was so beset with the routines that he never got to the spiritual work he intended to do. The terrible thing is that so much of this seems essential—it has to do with our parochial reports and a good showing—it puts a premium on the American hustler and advances his ecclesiastical chances—and only when we get off and take a good look at our "successes" do we see how great failures they really are. When we compound this with the failures of other people, knowing how general the situation is, we tend to settle into our mediocrity with complacency; and when we hear and see true spiritual power anywhere, we either refuse to recognize it, or to face the judgment which is implied against our institutionalism. We simply make an idol of the Church when we leave out the fellowship of the Holy Spirit, the fire and the life. Dr. Carl Bates, of Amarillo, Texas, says concerning our church programs, "If God calls His Holy Spirit out of the world, about 95 per cent of what we are doing would go on and we would brag about it"; he asks the uncomfortable question, "What are you doing that you can't get done unless the *power of God* falls on your ministry?"

In place of a passion for souls, we have substituted a passion for statement. We have made idols out of carefully chosen words. Scholarly men will grope learnedly and mannerly after a precise word or statement, to which no one can take exception; and this will be incorporated into a long report which few will read, but the writing of which has taken the time of men who would write much more trenchantly, succinctly, and convertingly if they had spent that same time working with unchanged and unconvinced people. No one can object to getting one's sights straight and taking a right aim: but one must ask to see some fruits of these things in concrete action. These messages and statements are often profoundly true and at times moving: but how many laymen could be persuaded to read them? A young minister says that the seminary taught him the answers to the questions, but he can't make his people ask the questions to which these things are the answers! We are loaded with words divorced from living realities, with truths unrelated to experience, with principles disconnected from persons, with programs irrelevant often to their own spoken aims. The statement of our dreams is often tremendous: but where is the implementation?

We shall not go forward under the leadership of the Holy Spirit until we repent, individually, as clergy, as parishes, as whole Communions. The Church as God gave and intended it is glorious: it is the Body of Christ. The Church as man has mishandled it is often tragic and unworthy of its name. We must repent of our decency without dynamic, of our programs, our failure to have time for individuals, our failure to mobilize our lay people, our failure to persuade them to tithe. We must repent of gambling for such small stakes when the Church is out to save the world. The Communists put us on the spot: they know what they believe, they have a plan for the world, and they don't care what it costs them personally to get it accomplished. Someone will say to me, "Do you mean that a lot of faithful, hard-working, churchgoing people are still outside the life in the Holy Spirit that Christ wants them to have?" The answer must be: precisely, and there will be no true repentance on our part until we face the fact that this means *you* and *me*.

Let us turn to some possible ways by which again we may give greater access to the Holy Spirit for the infusion of the Church.

We must learn and keep ever in mind the difference between the organic and the organizational in the life of the Church. Many think that if we set up a good organization, with by-laws, a budget, and the right people behind it, and say a prayer or two, the thing will happen. This is the picture of nine-tenths of what we do. But it happens that this is not how Jesus worked. He talked to people, in groups and one by one, drew them to Him in faith and fellowship, took them with Him where they could watch His outpoured power, fashioned them into a working brotherhood, trained them to do the same things He did, sent the Holy Spirit upon them by promise, and then physically departed. He worked organically. The organizational thinks in terms of administration, finance, committees, ways and means. The organic knows that all that really matters is the impact of God on people, their interpersonal relations with each other, the effect of faith and the new life upon others on the outside. When all this really gets under way, of course it can and will use organization and forms, as a live, growing tree will make a trunk and bark: but one can't take a dead post, nail bark on it, pump sap into it, and expect to get leaves or fruit on it. The churches are often a mass of more or less lifeless, though very busy, organization. A friend of mine says we suffer from "committee-ized Christianity." We can meet so impersonally on our committees, and so powerlessly, so far as any spiritual output is concerned. We who are responsible for the leadership of the Church need time for people. We need accessibility. We need informality. We need the human touch. We need the dynamic of experience, of fellowship, of witness, and of joy. We need the Holy Spirit.

For another thing, we must come by a deeper conception of conversion. We usually conceive of it, if we think of it at all, in terms of belief or of conduct, thus making the mind and the will central to it. I think we need to recognize that Christian conversion, in the powerful days of the Early Church, consisted of two things that seemed to happen at the same time: Jesus was risen from the dead, and they came to believe in Him as the Divine Son of God and their Savior. At the same time took place their immersion into the fellowship of the Church, characterized chiefly by the current of power running through it all the while, which was the life and presence of the Holy Spirit. This involved not the mind only and the will, but the emotions, the imagination, what we should call the subconscious. These people were released into God and into each other. The reason why it will always be true to say *extra ecclesiam nulla salus* (outside the church there is no salvation) is that no one can experience this kind of deliverance apart from the Beloved Company. I am saved by Christ in part through you, and you through me. As we are received and accepted in this company, grow and develop in it, as a child does in a home, we keep finding Him anew through one another, serving Him best when serving with one another. To be saved is to be immersed in the stream of the Holy Spirit, buoyed and carried along by Him. On a river or an ocean, we must do something to propel ourselves; but the great force is the buoyancy of the water itself. It is so with the Spirit. We must let this stream of Grace do for us what we can never do by reason nor by effort. Conversion must get through us like humidity gets through a house with the windows open on a muggy day—it is everywhere, in your clothes, in stamps in the desk drawer, even in the rugs! Conversion which only reaches our thoughts, or our outward conduct, is very rudimentary conversion. Conversion is a live, transforming, never-ending process. It is the life of the Holy Spirit in the soul.

In the new day of the Spirit, I am sure that Sacraments are going to count for much more than they usually do among Protestants, as I am sure that conversion is going to count for much more than it usually does among Catholics. The reason why some of us say more about conversion than about Sacraments is not lack of conviction about Sacraments; it is the profound conviction that most of us are not converted enough to know what Sacraments are all about. Unconverted people going steadily to the Sacraments are almost bound to make idols of them. We do not want to strengthen people in their half-commitment, or encourage them to believe that all they need is more of what they have, and further progress down the road. Some of them aren't on the road at all, never have been. Growth does not begin until there has been some kind of death, and a true beginning of growth, e.g., the seed. I have a few acorns in my desk: unless they go into the ground, die, and begin to live in a new tree, they will never grow. The conversion is going into the ground. The growth begins when the new life is started.

What we need is *both* conversion and sacramental grace. Some of us are very familiar with the story of the two apostles going down to Samaria to administer what we call Confirmation to those who had only been baptized. One would think, to hear some Episcopalians talk, that Confirmation was all that interested the apostles. But read on a few more verses: "When Peter and John had given their clear witness and spoken the Word of the Lord, they set out for Jerusalem, preaching the Good News to many Samaritan villages as they went" (Acts 8:25, Phillips). There was no conflict for them. Faith came by hearing the Word. Faith led to being received into the Church, where the Sacraments are found. Bishop Walter J. Carey, a vigorous High Churchman, said that Sacraments are equally necessary with Conversion, but logically subsequent because, unless a person has been converted to Christ, there is no reason why he should wish to make any use of the Christian Sacraments.[6]

I think the churches must all find some better way of exposing people to the Gospel than most of us now employ. Neither the excitable revival, nor the pedestrian and routine "joining" of the Church, always manage to do this. Most people have never been with other people of relatively their own situation, who were seeking to live out a vigorous converted life. They hear pieces of the Gospel in church and in sermons, but they have seldom heard laymen talking in the contagious, infectious way that A.A.'s talk in their meetings: and it is from this that alcoholics in

[6] *Conversion, Catholicism and the English Church.*

need find their inspiration and new hope. This can hardly be done in a Sunday morning service, though more of it could be if ministers would tell more stories about contemporary people, and more often let laymen come in and tell their own stories. And most of our informal church meetings are not set at the level of the outsider or the inquirer or the pagan, but at the level of transacting the church's business, which may interest the already interested and caught, but certainly not the outsider. We need a new kind of meeting where people may be brought into contact with current Christian experience. We shall say more of these gatherings when we come to discuss the creation of small groups for discussion and prayer.

And we need an altogether different kind of conference or retreat. To be talked at continually for two days gives little opportunity to absorb or to ask questions. Merely to be silent for the same time, even under direction, may not give the opportunity for exchange which combines growth in experience with growth in fellowship. A conference needs a minimum of structure, and a maximum of liberty under the Spirit. Let a leader speak in an experiential way, or get others to do it, so that the level is the level of experience, not merely of ideas; then call for a period of Quiet and waiting on God; then let people express what has been coming to them. When this ravels out into more talk, begin again. We must have spiritually resourceful people on hand, and give new people plenty of chance to break in and ask questions. When the Spirit is present, and the human moderator keeps things moving in one general direction, so that there is not mere chaos of expression, great things happen.

This is especially true about clergy conferences. The learned addresses of scholars need to be greatly supplemented, if not supplanted, by simple expressions of need and of discovery on the part of the men themselves. Again, experience is the order of the day—not ideas, not the carrying out of a tight, prearranged schedule—but events, with the Holy Spirit given free rein to carry matters in His own direction. I have seen Him more often kept out altogether by stiff conformity to schedule than by a few unexpected and informal excursions into the unarranged! We held such a conference not very long ago: the only speakers were lay people, and the listeners were clergy! The tables were turned clear around. Two groups of young laymen, one talking about the effects of faith at the downtown level, the other about life in the parish, a talk on prayer and prayer groups by my wife, and the tape recording of a brilliant witness by "The Late Liz" (which tape, by the way, is available), were the things that set the pace and level. Then the parsons were free to talk, ask questions, and contribute experience. The time of prayer at the end of the two days, in which everyone took part without being urged to do so, was a memorable experience of power for us all.

One of the men writes, "I've always looked for fellowship with the positive element in the Christian ministry, and this was certainly it! I have had a deep fear and aloofness as to ministers, because the ones I knew did so much to 'act' the part. Now that I am a minister, the fear is still hard for me to dislodge. Our meeting last week did a lot to free me from this." Another says, "I am so sure that what happened to me there last week is something God did, ranking with my conversion fourteen years ago in importance. I really do not understand why, having heard about the Holy Spirit all my life, it was in *this* conference that He has become a part of my personal experience. Part of my joy is that the theology I've been hewing out, with the encouragement and prodding of faculties at several of the best seminaries in the country, and other individuals, does not conflict at any point with this new thing that has happened to me, but rather is confirmed by it. My experience of the Holy Spirit does not begin to compare with that of others about whom I have read, but it has been a liberating thing for me these last few days." It is a joyous thing to hear what some of these men say of continuing experiences after they got home.

A layman who had attended much the same kind of conference writes, "I'd like to let you know how much the conference meant to me. Not so much the structural program as instructional conversation led me to make my initial commitment and brought a real turning point in my life. It is really joyous to see oneself grow in faith. I am very glad to have come out of a rather conservative stage in which I restrained my mind a bit, for now my faith-relationship to the living God is strong enough so I can work out doctrinal doubts within it. It is a great unshackling to realize that there is no virtue in accepting what is false for any reason, but that the Lord God demands that we question and seek the truth whatever the cost, and then speak the truth in love."

In most churches, there is no occasion where response to a new visitation by the Holy Spirit may be expressed. Suppose a person has come through a great trial and found the help of God: should this always be kept to oneself? Suppose one has heard an address or read a book that put into effect a new resolve: how is this to be maintained and to grow if no other human being knows anything of it? The best many can say, after a service and sermon that have really moved them, is to tell the minister at the door, "I enjoyed your sermon." Well, sometimes the sermons have not been of the 'enjoying' kind. They bared the preacher's soul and told blunt truth and got down to realities. We must take the will for the deed: maybe this word about 'enjoying the sermon' is a modest way of expressing an inward change. But is it too modest? For many of us, going to church is getting a little bit changed sometimes: how badly do we need a real turning, a great decision, a fresh surrender! One recognizes the limitations of services which give people a chance to 'come forward,' or register some decision in another way; but one must also recognize the limitations of churches that never give people such an opportunity at all. Dr. Alan Walker, reporting on Billy Graham's meetings in Australia, says, "As people surged forward to register 'decisions for Christ' many a Christian minister recognized in his heart that he had been unfaithful, content merely to influence people rather than to seek a commitment of the will." [7]

This leads us to comment on the necessity for something beside ordinary church services or study groups to waken and arouse our people. If I had not gone to Northfield, as boy and young man, and seen there the giants of fifty years ago—Robert E. Speer, John R. Mott, and others—I don't think I should ever have got past an Episcopalian parish religion. I am grateful for the latter, grateful that I still participate in the Church at a local level; but one could hardly have said that it was very fiery or thrilling or had much relevance to the world situation. Why do

[7] *The Christian Century*, July 15, 1959.

many of our people read *Unity?* Because it suggests the availability of real power and experience. Retreats, conferences, exposure to outstanding personalities, special meetings and missions, may all have their place in putting more fire into the practice of religion. These may all be channels through which the Spirit wants to work.

One clergyman said recently that he feels the Church can go forward only as we develop an understanding and redemptive fellowship between clergy and laity. He says the clergy cannot carry the load of their work and at the same time be put on pedestals by parishioners, only to fall off through some human limitation or fault and judged and criticized by their people. This makes the clergy self-righteous when they stay on the pedestal, and the people self-righteous when the clergy fall off the pedestal, unless a mutually redemptive fellowship is in some way made a working and living reality, and not consigned to the limbo of a pious wish.

The Church, and the churches, must always be on the alert for genuine movements of the Spirit arising in their midst and without the institutional framework. The Holy Spirit seems to find men and women with some creative gift, and set in motion through them something that fills a human need and rounds out the total life of the Church. Not all of these are of equal value and soundness. No one of them can represent all there is in the Church. In a sense, the Church is, among other things, the sum of these persons and their gifts and the movements these may create. The red tape of ecclesiastical authority and organization has throttled many of them, and either refused to give them standing room or, as Dr. Van Dusen says, taken them under the organizational wing and cut the distinctive life out of them. The Holy Spirit is at once more selective than we, and apparently more democratic. We must not judge of these things from our timidity, our laziness, our want of spiritual perceptiveness, nor—above all—from our feeling of being reproached by them—"threatened" is the current silly word for this. When, pray, did anybody ever meet a spiritual challenge to be different, to go farther for Christ, who did *not* feel "threatened" by it? God is trying to say something to His Church through these men and movements we often think of as upstarts. The Church is emphatically *not* that old brick building on the corner, nor its system of tiresome routines: the Church is the company that is filled with the Holy Spirit, and manifests the fruits of the Spirit. It is He, not we, who makes the choice of where, when, and through whom He will work.

The Church needs and must have many things—scholarship, physical equipment, ordered finance, well-planned services, up-to-date religious education—one can make a long list. But to think that all this list of assistances, let alone any one or two of them, is going to bring the awakening the Church needs today is sheer folly. Some people in my own Church get so excited about a little liturgical change, like having laymen carry forward the Bread and Wine with the money-offering, so that the priest presents them all at once as a symbol of the offering of the congregation themselves. It is a fine bit of symbolism. But will this move the hardness of heart, or get at the profound determination in us to get our own way right in the midst of our religious profession, or bring us really into the stream of the Spirit? Personally I gravely doubt it. What the Church truly needs is the Holy Spirit, deep fellowship at the center of its life, and witness in life and words as its overflow.

I have been trying to say something of what I believe needs to happen, something of what might happen, something of what will happen if certain conditions are fulfilled. This comes first and last and always back to the door of the Church itself. When the Church has power, the world gets intrigued. When the Church has power, the world gets convicted. When the Church has power, the world gets converted. But no man can be the author of this, though one cannot but feel that tens of thousands of people praying for it and letting themselves be part of the channel of it would give the Holy Spirit the agents that He must want.

Let us pray deeply and often with this little ladder of affirmation and commitment:

I need the Holy Spirit
I want the Holy Spirit
I pray for the Holy Spirit
I wait for the Holy Spirit

8

The Holy Spirit and the Layman

There has been a good deal written and said about the growing importance of laymen in our time, and many of us have high hopes from this development. Some of it has been foolish talk, like a graduation speaker looking into the faces of some boys and girls who are receiving their diplomas, and calling youth "the hope of the world." It is going to take everything that ministers and laymen together can accomplish to move us much ahead: there is no greater wisdom inherent in laymen than in clergy. But there are more of them, and they can, and we pray will, make a distinctive contribution to the spiritual movement of our day. They are often closer than clergy to the human situations in which Christ is either exalted, or crucified again; and unless Christ's enterprise succeeds in such places, the Church is failing in its mission.

We are seeing more and more clearly that there must be a double movement for the laity: first a movement out of the world and into the Church; and then a movement out of the Church and back into the world again. It is not enough to get people to go to church: they are meant to carry into the fields of daily life and work the grace and Spirit they have found in church. This is a bridge which must rest on solidity at either end: a known Lord and Gospel, and a known world and job. A Gospel divorced from the inevitable anomalies of living and working cannot be a Christian Gospel; for the Christian Gospel began when "the Word was made flesh and dwelt among us," and typically God came into all the limitations and complexities of ordinary life. Our efforts to capture business and politics for God do not spring from sentimental idealism, they spring from the Incarnation itself. All life belongs to God and is intended to reflect Him.

There is a fine report to be had from the Department of Laity of the World Council of Churches, on the role of the laity in the life and ministry of the Church, which contains this paragraph: "Where is the Church's front? . . . That is, its service, its ministry to the world? Does the front not go right through the place you yourself occupy? Can one not say that the Church succeeds or fails in its ministry according to whether or not something is happening in the name of Jesus Christ in your sector of the activities of this world?"

"Something is happening in the name of Jesus Christ in your sector. . . ." There is a test for every Christian, layman or clergyman, man or woman.

The first question which arises is that of vocation. Those who most believe in God believe in His majestic creating and sustaining power in the vast universe; but also in His concern for the most minute details of life. If He has a will for the way we treat every human being, and the way we meet every situation, surely He has a will for the whole of our life—where we shall spend it, what shall be our field of activity, how we shall prosecute this work. It is common to think that only ministers and missionaries are meant to have a "call"—being a banker, or a salesman, or a factory worker is too mundane a matter to call for God's attention. But this takes these fields out of God's hands, and draws a line between "sacred" and "secular" which denies the Incarnation and eventually sullies common life and activity. We need to pray as much about becoming a lawyer as about becoming a monk. We must put our natural fears and desires in God's hands as much as we can, and ask for His will. If this thought comes to us late in life, when we are in too deep to change (or think we are), then I think we need to pray again, and ask whether thinking it too late to change is valid or an excuse—many men do change their occupations in middle, and some in much later, life. Let us not take the vocational question out of God's hands, and keep it solely in our own. And when we have done the best we can to find His plan, then let us do what St. Paul tells us in I Corinthians 7:17, "Let every one lead the life which the Lord has assigned to him, and in which God has called him" (RSV).

This—like all Christian precepts—is so much easier to say than to do. No human thing is free from compromise and anomaly. Let no man claim nor think that the Church is, either: I have seen as much politicking and undercutting and self-seeking and ambition in the workings of the Church as in the most dog-eat-dog business practices. When a man or woman dares to stand against any of these things, even when they are approached with the utmost of patience and tact, misunderstanding and even reprisal may be expected in return. An act of integrity and a word of truth and challenge are more than a piece of personal courage: by implication they judge business, and *this* business, and no one involved enjoys that. When a family and a livelihood are involved, the threat of disapproval or dismissal is serious. Moreover, we cannot expect individuals to abandon altogether the natural seeking for status which Barbara Ward says is "unavoidable and unquenchable in Western society."[1] It is cheap and easy to stand in a safe pulpit and give voice to fine aspirations: it is something else to have the courage, the patience, and the ingenuity to apply the principles of Christian faith and practice, even in a modest degree, to active life as it is carried on in the world today.

But if we begin by calling it an impossible task, we are whipped before we start. As there have been lives, families, communities, and churches where some real measure of the Spirit was present, so there have been and are business situations in which God can work because the men involved let Him work through them. I am reasonably sure that God usually comes into a business or political situation through human beings and human relations; and that the place where we meet and do business with people is the place where we welcome God in, or banish Him out. This calls for faith and courage, but, almost as

[1] *Faith and Freedom*, p. 221.

much, for ingenuity and good nature. For "how" one does this, the spirit in which it is done, may determine how far we get, even more than does our daring. The crusader on a white horse in business, with banners flying and slogans ringing, will find himself alone and unappreciated. But one who knows himself and his own emotions to be the great problem, and seeks to let God control him, and through prayer guide his mood and action, may be surprised at the response he will receive. We must not be downed by compromises in the past. I know a man who accepted a job with the pretty clear understanding that he would "pipe down" on his religious convictions; and for a time he was a little like an extinct volcano. But he is not so today, and there is a sharp spiritual edge to his life that may cut cleaner than words can do.

In addition to this, we must be mindful—we who can give our full time to spiritual matters—of the time pressures that are on men in business and the professions. Many of them have a great deal more leisure than they ever think of using for God; but let me testify that some of our men in Pittsburgh are having to watch out that they give a right amount of time and energy to their jobs and to their families, when their spiritual activity is so constant and so demanding. There is no witness in a job poorly done or a family emotionally neglected. If men are truly in the stream of the Spirit nothing will be neglected or overdone. But who does not know tense moments when his duty does not seem clear, and when he must withdraw for a private session with the Lord and maybe some of his friends, to get his sights reset, his vision clear, and his tensions quieted?

Anybody can retreat from daily work life, into churchwork, and seem very bold and courageous in an area where all this is accepted. Many do. They often know it is a retreat and springs from cowardice. It begs the question whether "something is happening in the name of Jesus Christ *in your sector*." That is where the real warfare is on, that is where victory is won, or defeat is experienced.

Not long ago I attended a large high school commencement. It is in an area where 80 per cent of the boys and girls are Negroes. In the things that were said by the student speakers and by the principal, one felt a strong spiritual undercurrent that was plainly the basis for such good spirit at the social level, and such good work at the academic. I found that the principal felt deeply the spiritual responsibility of his office. And I found that one of the women teachers is an ardent Christian, who has brought to bear an indirect but strong influence on her pupils. A teacher's job cannot be used as an evangelistic soapbox: but one can let his prayers and his faith permeate what he does so that those about him feel it. And this is what she does.

There is a remarkable organization called the Fellowship of Christian Athletes. They call their movement a "program and movement to confront athletes—and through them the youth of the nation—with the challenge and adventure of the Christian Life." Six hundred and twenty-five of them gathered at Estes Park, Colorado, in August 1959, with a hundred and fifty turned away for want of space. Day after day we listened to men like Don Moomaw, Don Meredith, Bob Feller, Charley Milstead, Bob Richards, Bud Held, Bob Pettit, Dan Towler, and coaches "Biggie" Munn, Dick Harp, Paul Dietzel, Frank McGuire, Don Faurot, and Ben Martin, speak and witness concerning Jesus Christ in relation to sport and athletics. This movement has seized on a great idea: to capitalize on the popularity of well-known athletic figures and bring them before audiences of undergraduates and high school students. It is a "natural." These men are learning to use their jobs and reputations for Christ.

Speaking to the graduating class of Harvard University on June 7, 1959, President Nathan Pusey said, "The finest fruit of serious learning should be the ability to speak the word God without reserve or embarrassment." The change of spiritual climate which has taken place in recent years in that university is well known. One cannot but feel that it stems from the personal faith and courage of the president, who is a Christian and makes no bones about it. I suppose he holds the most eminent academic position on this continent. Properly he uses his right as an individual to express his faith; but his influence goes in unimaginably distant directions. Why don't hundreds more do it?

I think of the steady, quiet impact of my friend David Griffith on the men in the Homestead Works of United States Steel, and many others outside it. His spiritual intensity and concern is not a whit less evident in the mill than when he is in church, or speaking in a meeting. His concern for people about him, his constant prayer to be led and used, the naturalness with which he makes it plain that the adventure of faith is for him seeking to stay always in the stream of the Holy Spirit, give the lie to those who say religion is for Sunday only.

The philosophy behind such witnessing cannot be better put than it is by Martin Buber, when he speaks of "Enoch . . . a cobbler, and with each stitch of his bodkin as it sewed the upper leather and the sole together, he joined together God and His Shekinah." [2] There is something unforgettable about that parallel, of God and the "upper leather," and His Shekinah and "the sole." It reminds us that religion is not idealism, but realism plus faith; that if we let the horizontal line represent life and facts, and the vertical line represent God and faith, religion goes into effect just at the right angle where faith meets fact. This is where things happen in translating the will of heaven into the ways of earth.

What about the relation between laymen and clergy in all this? Ideally, as we have said, the relation should be that of a coach to the players. Without a coach, there is no team; and without a team, a coach hardly exists. A minister usually knows his way amid the truths of the faith, whatever he may know of practical business life; and he ought to know something, too, of human nature, and the way it works in general. He will not know much of the special problems of particular professions or jobs. He must not, therefore, eschew contact with men at the downtown level, but let them teach him of the realities of business as perhaps he can teach them of the realities of faith. He should be with them in a crucible of experience, trying, learning, failing, trying again. He must not expect laymen to live in the stream of the Spirit, and draw others into it, unless he tries to do the same thing himself. There is a memorable picture of the Ideal Shepherd in St. John 10; and at the 4th verse it says of him that, having driven all his flock outside (not allowing them to stay in the safety of the sheepfold), "he goes in front of them himself" (Phillips). Having pushed them out from behind, he then leads

[2] *To Hallow This Life,* p. 59.

them from in front. He gives them the lead. The minister should always do that.

He has another function: to nourish and conserve what he or others have been used of the Spirit to set in motion. There is a teaching and feeding responsibility that is his. He must be especially careful as he seeks to weave together what another outside his Church may have given one of his people, and what the Church itself wants to give them. Clergy who pooh-pooh the impulse from without as being dubious, and give the impression that now "The Church" will give them the straight of it all, come perilously near blaspheming the Spirit. But clergy who are thankful for whatever the Spirit has done, and are now eager to give all the teaching and help that the Church can provide, are essential in this whole process of conversion, growth, and training. In 1760 John Wesley wrote his brother Charles that Cornwall had suffered miserably from his (John's) long absence, "and the unfaithfulness of the preachers." Evidently these were men with so little spiritual power that they hadn't the grace nor the concern to help sustain what Wesley had begun. When someone converted, say, in a Billy Graham campaign, is turned over to a local minister, who gives him no counsel nor concern, the local minister is in no position to say that these conversions "do not last." Of course they don't if he doesn't give the people what they need to grow!

The Holy Spirit does not always work on our customary assumption that it is clergy that "give" in spiritual matters, and lay people that "take." Sometimes He works just the other way around. There is a clergyman who today is exercising an expectant, Spirit-filled ministry, reaching individuals, incorporating them into training groups, and helping them to witness. He did not learn this in seminary. The spark came to him from a lay woman in his congregation, who in talking with him one day, asked whether he had ever surrendered his life to Christ. He was somewhat surprised, and began talking about his call to the ministry, and his profound theological belief in Christ. She said, "I asked you just the question, Are you surrendered to Christ?" And he had to say in all honesty, "No, I am not." She kept talking with him until he went down on his knees and let go. From that hour, power began quietly pouring into him and through him into lives about him.

The next thing is training. For growth means little if it is merely a selfish growth. All vital movements make converters out of their converts. People come as fields, they should go out as forces. They must be helped to see and see through the very processes by which they have themselves been converted, so that they may be used of the Spirit to reach yet others. There are techniques, methods, ways, a "how" in these matters that can be learned to some degree by exposure. And this means the need for training groups, where the theoretical training and the actual impact on people are joined together simultaneously. Here is the place where many churches are most woefully lacking. Accepting people's natural humility, which says they are not ready to go out without a great deal more training, we may keep them for months, even years, studying, learning, absorbing, taking in—and they never get to the last step of giving it away! Dr. Erik Erikson, in his book *Young Man Luther*, speaks of the elements in the success of the Chinese Communists in thought reform: "removal from family and community and isolation from the outer world; restriction of sensory intake and immense magnification of the power of the word; lack of privacy and radical accent on the brotherhood; and, of course, joint devotion to the leaders who created and represented the brotherhood." [3] He says that this "indoctrination must be incisive in its deprivations, and exact in its generous supply of encouragement." Of course, this smells of totalitarianism and dictatorship: but where have we ever seen a Christian counterpart to it where any such sacrifice and discipline were even suggested, and accepted by the trainees?

Dr. Van Dusen has called for "a new Protestant Reformation," suggesting three programs: (1) interdenominational guilds of Christian lawyers, bankers, physicians, teachers, industrialists, labor officers, and others to analyze ethical problems and opportunities in each profession; (2) creating city-wide groups of Christian laymen to resolve issues that defy Christian standards and cry for Christian judgment and action; (3) development of

[3] Pp. 333, 334.

united fellowship, united thought, united planning, and, above all, united action by laymen's organizations.[4] These are mighty proposals: I seriously question how many laymen we have who are mature enough to provide such leadership. They will need deep commitment personally, and real training, before they can function in this fashion. Back of any large and wholesale efforts there must lie the personal dealing without which no one is spiritually trained nor ready. Baron von Hügel said that "*usually* one thoroughly trained spiritual soul has in the background another trained spiritual soul as its trainer."[5] And Bishop Amritanand has said that in the mass movements of India he found it invariable that those who were greatly used were people to whom at some time a great deal of personal attention had been given.[6] This training should bring laymen to the place where, as time goes on, they can (1) lead audibly in prayer, (2) bring another person to decision, (3) speak and witness in a meeting, (4) lead a meeting introducing other speakers, (5) conduct a continuing small group, and (6) affect a whole situation.

All of this concerns building and tending the personal foundations of faith. Some will ask: Where does the social application of all this come in? It begins to come in the moment any man or woman starts treating another in as nearly Christian a fashion as possible. It proceeds organically from this—not from abstract theories only, but from living human relations. One cannot be and continue in fellowship with another while being indifferent to his economic and social status, and without seeking to improve these, both for him and for other people in a similar situation. There is no antithesis between personal religion and social conscience: the need is for personal religion to get deep enough to affect the whole of life and thinking, and for the social conscience to realize that when it is divorced from spiritual motivation it always risks driving toward man's domination of man. Listen to this word from Thomas R. Kelly's classic, *A Testament of Devotion*: "John Woolman, the Quaker tailor of Mt. Holly, New Jersey, resolved so to order his outward affairs,

[4] *The New York Times*, Feb. 15, 1958.
[5] *Letters to a Niece*, p. 111.
[6] See my book, *The Church Alive*, p. 34.

so to adjust his business burdens, that nothing, absolutely nothing would crowd out his prime attendance upon the Inward Principles. And in this sensitizing before the inward altar of his soul, he was quickened to see and attack effectively the evils of slaveholding, of money-loaning, of wars upon the Indians." [7] There is more heart-searching concerning the social implications of the Christian message going on now among businessmen than ever before; and more quiet, almost invisible forces moving through them to this end. Sheer self-interest is a powerful opponent of this, but I am quite sure that steady progress is being made.

One would think, to hear some people talk, that the lay movement were a modern thing. It would be strange if the Church had to wait almost two thousand years for it to emerge! But this seems not to be the case. From the first laymen were involved in the direct communication of the Word. It is evident from the closing chapters of I Corinthians that speaking in tongues and prophesying were common, and that they were done by the ordinary men of the Church. St. Paul does not forbid speaking in tongues, even does it himself, but he says that this does not edify the other hearers as prophesying does. He makes prophesying the great gift, saying, "I want you all to speak in tongues, but even more to prophesy. . . . You can all prophesy one by one, so that all may learn and all be encouraged." And he adds something of great significance: "and the spirits of prophets are subject to prophets" (I Cor. 14:5, 31-32, RSV). This seems to mean that no one speaks entirely on his own; he speaks as of the company. What is given to him to say is personal, his own; but it must edify the hearers, and it must be in line with the message of the whole Church—a wise, most wise, provision!

But what was the content of these prophesyings? There was then no New Testament to speak from. These ordinary believers were scarcely sufficiently schooled to offer theological instruction. The prophesying must have been their own personal witness and testimony, the inspired, relevant word given. They were, I profoundly believe, sharing with others their own Spirit-given experiences. Prophesying was not preaching, in our modern sense, for ordinary believers were engaged in it; it was testi-

[7] P. 34.

mony, witness, the sharing of up-to-date personal experience. We cannot doubt that the presence of this personal prophesying was a powerful contributing factor to the life and strength of the Early Church. We certainly cannot doubt that this factor has been almost completely lacking in most of our modern churches. The Rev. Claxton Monro, rector of St. Stephen's Church, Houston, Texas, to whom I owe directly the thought in this paragraph, believes that, as the Bible was the center of authority in the Reformation of four hundred years ago, the Spirit-filled community of believers will be the center of authority and the channel of power in the reformation of our day. Laymen are, of course, the large majority of this prophesying company. And the so-called "lay movement" turns out to have begun as an essential part of the Early Church!

There are plenty of ministers, not all belonging to "catholic"-oriented churches, either, who quash any lay activity beyond the support of plans which clergy have made, and in which they exercise practically the only spiritual leadership. Lay activity ought to keep itself in line with the minister's parish policy, and he should be brought in on it, even if this involves a patient process of drawing the minister along by inclusion and by loyalty to him in his parish leadership. One can understand the clergyman's desire not to let loose "wild men" among his people; but he must be warned that, if his suppression of lay activity goes too far, he may well have a shell for a church, and he may drive these enthusiastic laymen to go elsewhere. Not all of these spontaneous uprisings are necessarily from God; but some clergy think every one of them is pretty nearly of the devil. This seeks to box the Holy Spirit in church forms and church routines--it gives Him no chance for a fresh, creative break-through which may be exactly what *the* Church, and what *this* church, needs. The final authority in the Church must be the Holy Spirit. We do well to heed His Voice through a constituted church authority, and we do well to remember that sometimes these men do not speak as they are moved by the Holy Spirit, but from fear, from jealousy, from powerlessness. As they need to keep close to the Holy Spirit in order to know "the mind of Christ," so do lay people need to keep close to Him in order to recognize Him wherever He is and through whomsoever He speaks. This obviously calls for a maturity, a selflessness, a search for the Holy Spirit, that go far deeper than anything we have often had. Those who make either Church or Bible all that we need confine the Holy Spirit to the past. Those who say and believe that He is contemporary, and must be heeded by us today as He deals with present-day individuals and companies, must be very guarded that the Holy Spirit, rather than self will, is the motivating force.

Yet we must deal with the Holy Spirit as He has shown Himself to be. He is not confined to any instruments created in the past, though He goes on using them. Indeed, I think He *will find* people to work through in fresh ways, whatever we say or do to limit Him. While we labor ponderously to prove an ancient point, the Holy Spirit has leaped like fire into another place. We cannot keep Him down! And we cannot deny His Presence where His fruits are manifest.

In 1857 and 1858 an awakening broke out in New York which was led almost entirely by laymen, touched off by the commercial crash and panic of 1857. A group of New York businessmen began noonday meetings for prayer in a Fulton Street church. Soon the gatherings overflowed into other buildings, and by the spring of 1858 twenty daily prayer meetings were being held all over the city. It began to spread, and soon every large town had its meetings, services, and columns of newsprint telling of what was happening. Bernard A. Weisberger, who tells this story,[8] goes on to say, "Defenders of the Revival were elated that in a time of crisis men would turn from their ledgers to God. They missed a significant fact, however. There was also a grasping for something familiar, established—something which could be managed without special guidance. The technique was so stabilized that there could be a revival without revivalists." And it seems that the technique was nothing more than the one familiar to all as the common factor in these awakenings: personal conversion, prayer, exchange of experience; and fellowship, in small groups; and witness by life and by word outside. The technique will not produce awakening, but it does seem to offer the Holy Spirit an avenue on which He can come in.

[8] *They Gathered at the River,* pp. 148-49.

9

How to Start a Group

It has been my belief for several years that the surest sign of spiritual awakening in our time is the emergence of the small spiritual group. It is as if, in a day of widespread loneliness and fear, the Holy Spirit were saying to us that the characteristic manifestation of His life and power would not be just in changed individuals, but in individuals found in relation to other individuals from the first. These meet under hundreds of different names and auspices, but they all belong, more or less, to one spiritual family: they seem to "know" each other when members of different groups meet; and I think that they may come more nearly representing the ecumenical movement, in its local, lay and grass-roots aspects, than any other sign of our time. They are, I deeply believe, an organic part of the Church, though not to be taken as a substitute for its usual worship and work. C. S. Lewis said more than a dozen years ago that the widespread interest in religion is "precisely what we call a fashion" and that whatever fashion gives, fashion may also withdraw: "the real conversions will remain, but nothing else will. In that sense, we may be on the brink of a real, permanent Christian revival: but it will work slowly and surely in small groups." [1]

These are nothing new in the life of the Church. Even in the ancient Jewish church there were small societies of friends who

[1] From *Cherwell,* an Oxford University magazine, 1947.

met weekly for devotion and charity: such a group was called a *chaburah.* Jesus and His Twelve would have formed such a *chaburah,* different from others only in the exceptionally close bond that drew them to their Leader and the independent attitude of the Leader toward accepted religious authorities.[2] One cannot miss the significance of the Twelve, in searching for ways to vitalize the Church of our own day; and again and again across the Christian centuries men have emerged with a burning fire in their hearts, who drew others about them; and through these groups have often come the impulse and means of awakening. If such groups will act as a kind of spearhead of awakening, strive constantly to be humble and teachable, and let the Holy Spirit be the Strategist that forms them all into "an exceeding great army" under His leadership alone, there is literally no telling what might happen in our day.

People sometimes say or write me, "How do you organize one of these small groups?" And the answer is, You can't organize them, any more than you can organize a love affair or a great poem. Groups are organic, i.e., they come about through the impact of life upon life. You can bring together a dozen spiritual-minded people, and nothing of any significance may happen at all. We Americans are, someone has said, the "eating-est, meeting-est" people in the world. Merely being together may be superficial and unsatisfying. Dr. Harry Stack Sullivan says, "I hope that you begin to get a notion of what I mean by pseudo-social ritual: in this case, each person is busily engaged with people, but nothing particularly personal transpires." [3] In such encounters, we are hardly dealing with persons as persons, but rather as objects—"it" rather than "he" or "she." This lies behind the loneliness of the crowd, the aching emptiness which we seek to meet by fellowship, but often fail to meet because we do not let ourselves become and be persons with each other. It takes awhile to know people well enough to touch on spiritual matters. One never knows where the Holy Spirit may come into a relationship or a company, and give it His own stamp of meaning and power. Perhaps the first question is not whether *we* want to start a group, but whether He does? If He does, He

[2] Dom Gregory Dix, *The Shape of the Liturgy,* p. 50.

[3] *The Interpersonal Theory of Psychiatry,* p. 306.

must ordinarily find someone who is open to such direction and leadership. It does not take great saints, else none of us would be so used; but it takes people with spiritual purpose and the beginnings of spiritual experience. Let us remember: everybody was once a beginner, perhaps a very inept beginner. If the will and intention are there, and prayer, God can use you.

It will be well to sit in on other groups, and see what "goes" and what does not, what is effective and what is not, to watch for good and poor procedures, to absorb experience at second hand. Perhaps you will say something yourself and participate, in which case you will learn more. You will notice how people sit with reasonable comfort and informality; light and air are important. The leader will be more a moderator than a chairman, with warmth and welcome toward everyone, enabling them soon to know one another through communication. Perhaps there will be a brief introduction of any new person, better if he will introduce himself. Whoever leads will not dominate the group too much, but will keep the strings lightly in his hands. There will be the play of natural humor, and the seriousness will come through a kind of lightness. It may all begin with a period of quiet, and there will be times in the meeting, perhaps, when no one will say anything: this can be a "living silence," not a "dead silence," if people are praying and keeping open. There may be a theme to the meeting, or it may begin with a short Bible study, or someone may be there as a visitor who should be given more than the usual time to speak. Something may be mentioned—a grave illness, an important appointment, a crisis in world affairs—that will call for immediate prayer. Let it all be done naturally, evolving rather than being manipulated. Sometimes it is well to go right round the circle, giving each a chance for a personal word, but pressing no one.

None can predict the times nor furnish the occasions for some deep break-through of the Spirit, in a felt unity, in a given corporate mind, in a joyous closeness of spirit, in an awareness of outpoured power. It is far more important to be yourself, and admit your fears or self-consciousness about the meeting, than to try to appear adequate or experienced. If others are to feel free to say what is on their hearts, the lead will have to be given by the more experienced people, but they must not monopolize it. Arguments about ideas will be deftly shelved, and the substance of the meeting will be shared experiences. It is well to have a stopping place, so that people know that after an hour, or an hour and a half, the meeting will end.

You must remember that this may be the first experience someone present has ever had of feeling fully accepted by a group, of being able to say what he is feeling without fear of being misunderstood. For some it will be so new that it will take time for them to feel at home or to express themselves. But for many this is the Church in small and compassable form. Here true relationships can form and grow. Here partial or distorted or even completely false ideas can come out, and find corrective —not from a leader declaring in dogmatic fashion what the truth is, but from the speaker feeling always freedom to say what he thinks, but then to hear also what others think. This double experience, of feeling that the group is going somewhere, and yet has time for the mistakes and even at times the garrulousness of a newcomer, may work off more mental and emotional tie-ups in people concerning religion than reading a hundred books and listening to a thousand sermons. Amid some dubious ideas and experimentation in the communication of religion in modern days there is one core of solid truth: and that is that until religion begins to be relational, it is hardly to be called Christianity at all. The same Lord who said, "Love the Lord thy God . . ." said, "Love thy neighbor as thyself"; and one feels that if the two things could have been said simultaneously, He would have done it—not because God is not more important than anybody else, but because it is so truly difficult to be in communication with Him without being also in communication with some of His people.

The group cannot and will not do everything. Its strength will be in fairly direct proportion to what is happening to its members outside as well as inside the meetings. Before you can make a brick wall, you have got to have some bricks; and before you can get movement through a living group you have got to have a few people who are converted enough (or beginning to be) to want to be used. Some things should only be talked out between two persons, and those who are habitually attending meetings should watch for those who want to talk privately, make occasion for them, and give them time. As the dynamic group becomes the epitome of the Church, so one understanding person becomes the epitome of the group. There are problems in connection with the first decision, and there may be problems later on, which require personal dealing. Don't be afraid of such close contact with another: it will help you as well as him. As you move ahead in the life of the group, you will learn more and more of God's ways with people, of human nature, of human relationships. It always amazes me how quckly members of Alcoholics Anonymous pick up what they call "the program," and how deeply they understand it sometimes after only a few weeks' exposure to it, whereas there are Christians who have been members of the Church for ten, twenty, forty years, who never learn "the program." These groups are meant to help people learn that there is a program and to begin to follow it. The life of the group grows and deepens as the spiritual life of the people in it moves more and more from ideas to experience.

As there is no way to guarantee the unbroken flow of the Spirit in the Church or in a movement, so there is no way to guarantee the upward progress of the small group. It has been my experience that often a group is like a baby—it may be heavier at birth than soon after when it begins to lose. But as care and food and love are likely to ensure the continuation of the baby's life, so there are usually ways to continue the group. But there will be some week when it is good, some when it is less good, some when it is poor: Rufus Jones once said of a Quaker meeting he attended that it was "a new high in lows." [4] We have all been to such meetings. Maybe the group has served its purpose and should break up with its members going on to some other kind of formation. But many a group begins declining from recognizable causes: (1) it has gone "churchy," formal, "busy," and needs to come back under the simplicity of the Spirit; (2) it has gotten enmeshed in the technicalities of religion itself and forgotten its purpose through interest in its means; (3) there is no overflow into the lives of others outside the group, so it is self-centered and goes stale. These are remedi-

[4] Elizabeth Gray Vining, *Friend of Life*, p. 197.

able. Let the small, inner group that should be taking the main responsibility come together for two or three hours, or go on a retreat together, and wait on God, and then be honest with each other about what has come to them in prayer. Much self-correction can come from within the group, if its members will really wait on God in honest listening.

Sometimes a group should consist of men only, and it may meet downtown at breakfast, or at lunch, or after work. Sometimes a group should consist of women only, and meet at their convenience. Sometimes a group should be composed of husbands and wives, and will meet in the evening. There is good in shuffling the nature of the group at times. In general, I think women like to gather in groups that avowedly meet for prayer, but this propels them out into the lives of other people so that prayer issues in work. And men seem to meet best for the exchange of experience, study, and planning, but without prayer this soon becomes humanistic and stringy. The healthy group has its dimension of depth in devotion and prayer, and of width in work and in witness.

Let me give some instances of these small groups:

I heard of thirty businessmen in one city that meet once a week with an Arthur Murray dancing instructor, and try honestly to answer to each other the question, "What have we done during the last six days for the life of this town?"

A magazine editor, weary of the way Americans "talk, talk, talk" all day long, formed an unorganized league of silence, of persons who promised to take five minutes in the middle even of the busiest days, wherever they happened to be, to think and pray and "realize," by keeping absolutely still and quiet.

Another group of literary men met for years in one city each week for an hour of absolute silence: they came in silence, they stayed together in silence, and they departed in silence. They say sometimes the power was electric.

A young minister I know gets his college boys and girls together when they are home during vacation and talks about what things are *real* to them—whether these be things of beauty, or of pain, or of joy, or of God. Beginning with what is "natural," he quietly brings it round to what is "spiritual," so that they see that these are not necessarily two things, but two sides of one thing.

A clergyman attended a conference which I led and where we talked of these things. He writes me as follows, "Being to some degree skeptical about the things you told us in Washington—being quite candid—I was none the less sufficiently moved and concerned to give it a try. Yesterday afternoon a second group wound up twelve sessions on 'What Does It Mean To Be a Christian?' The first group of twenty-two consisted of vestrymen, wives, and church staff, and seemed to me a good place to start. A second group of younger couples was begun three weeks later and worked for over eight weeks for two hours each Sunday afternoon and Thursday night. This group began with twelve people and ended with fifty-seven. Numbers tell little but had I known eight years ago what God might accomplish through me, I am certain that I would have ventured more boldly long before. On the basis of our beginning here this spring, I am certain that if we clergy were a little less timid and expected more and asked for more, God would see that both we and our people would receive more. . . . Thank you for giving me a good jolt at just the moment it was most needed."

Another young clergyman, after spending a year in a suburban parish going through the routines, with nothing happening, wrote asking what he could do with his younger marrieds. I wrote and told him the story of our younger marrieds at Calvary Church, Pittsburgh, and he asked me to send him the book with which our course with them began. He ordered a dozen, and this was his first report: "Last Saturday we had our first meeting of the younger marrieds. Everyone was a little tense, including yours truly at first. But we went round the room telling a little about ourselves, then I gave them the story of why I thought we should be meeting. By then we had all relaxed and I gave them the copies of *How To Become a Christian.* We started in reading by paragraphs, and leaving the text for some forthright discussion. As time went on, some began to have a gleam in their eyes. One young mother unburdened her heart about the purposelessness of modern life facing our children. When the evening was over, something had happened . . . their appetite had been whetted. All unanimously agreed to meet again right after the holidays. I took the books back, saying I didn't want them to read ahead! Ten were on hand, including my wife and myself. I have great hopes. . . . One young man was full of questions and quite critical. He had a comment for every paragraph—i.e., 'I don't think the world is that bad!' Each succeeding paragraph tripped him up a little more, and by the end of the evening his presuppositions were fairly demolished. He ought to turn out to be a good one! . . . Keep us in your prayers."

Some young people of about college age in a suburban parish wanted to get going some young people's work. They invited us to bring along some of our own young adults. There was a fellow on hand with all the organizational answers, and I had to say to them straight out, "You must choose between an organization, and an organism. There are tens of thousands of young adult groups that are organizations, have a constitution and officers and programs, and never get beyond being a social group. If you want a spiritual organism, you begin a different way." They said they wanted the latter. After talking with them a while about groups in various places, I called on four of our own young adults. Very naturally and simply they told their own stories and how the group came up out of relationships. This opened up a recent university graduate in the group who said he had two Christian roommates who had really witnessed to him, but whom he had fended off: and now he knew he must get going. He and some of the others present decided to meet regularly for Bible study and the exchange of experience. A strong group has emerged from it.

Dr. Elton Trueblood, whose work with the "Yokefellows" is so widely known, says there are five elements in common that are found in these informal groups:

1. A primary emphasis on commitment.
2. An unequivocal belief in the "priesthood of all believers"—laymen have been ignored, then enlisted, and now must be transcended, so that there is a universal ministry of clergy and laymen together.
3. An emphasis on reality in fellowship.

4. An emphasis on work—daily work—at the job level.
5. An unapologetic acceptance of spiritual discipline.

In connection with his fifth point, I would suggest six parts of a Christian Rule of Life that are definite enough to constitute a real "discipline" yet not so onerous but what an ordinary person can keep them:

1. A commitment to Christ, made once and for all, but repeated each time I pray.
2. A definite time with God each day, if possible at the start of the day, consisting of Bible study, prayer, and meditation.
3. Weekly fellowship with other Christians, in the Church, and in a smaller company for mutual help.
4. A "tithe" gift (one tenth) of my income to God's work in the world.
5. An honest effort day by day to apply in my work and human relations Christian love, humility, truth, and faith.
6. A real effort, by life and by witness, to win others to Him, His way of life, and His Kingdom.

Faithful adherence to such a self-imposed rule of life will keep providing us with new truth and information; and if it is pursued even during what appear to us as dry periods (everyone has them), it will go far toward getting us out of them when the right time comes. The spiritual highways are strewn with the wrecks of lives that tried to live forever upon the fiery impulse of the initial experience. No one who is not prepared to settle down to the hard work of some steady spiritual discipline can look for growth or even survival.

The small group is no panacea. It may become ingrown and lose its power. But we cannot evade one thing that stares us in the face from the pages of the Gospels: Jesus gave a few men the best of His time, His attention, His training. The crowds heard Him, individuals one after another were healed, but the constant factor was "the twelve." It sometimes seems to us as if it were all going one way, and that is what *He* was giving to *them.* But was it so? I think that even He needed the reinforcement of their loyalty, the sight of their joy when they were being used, the help of their widening experience, and the meaningfulness of their love. The law of this kind of spiritual energy does not change. "Two or three gathered together in my name . . ." is the expectant situation. What the Holy Spirit can do with this, multiplied in many places, only the long future can tell.

10

The Holy Spirit and Ourselves

If the things we have been saying in this book are anywhere near the truth, we who say we believe in the Holy Spirit are capable of far greater achievements than have ever been seen. We know that we cannot command Him, and we know that He alone is capable of creating the world-wide awakening that is needed. But God has always worked through people. It would be difficult to believe that God is not ready to "pour out His Spirit upon all flesh," if only more of us were deeply available to Him. In one sense, the awakening is His business alone—in another sense, it is very much up to us. For, while we cannot bring about the awakening in our own strength, we can hold it back by our own refusals. We know all too well that it is tens of thousands of people just like ourselves, partially converted, partially trained, partially mobilized, but not "given" as we might and could be, that keep God's forces in the world running at such minimal strength and such slow pace. There is evidence enough (we have shown some of it in these pages) that ordinary people can move beyond their conventionalities, beyond their timidities, beyond even their own human capacities, and light fires about them, when they truly "let go." Someone writes me, "When you have been touched by the Holy Spirit and by fire, you never give up, you just give in."

The first personal call to us, then, is to a life of deepened conversion and self-surrender. This brings the whole matter right back to our own front doors. It is not "they" who are out of the life and power, it is "we"—no, it is "I." Between our greater psychological insight, and the effects of neo-Orthodox theology, some of us have so taken for granted our halfheartedness, our sinfulness, our having "no power of ourselves to help ourselves," that we have settled back into expected failure and unchallenge-able discouragement. In the effort to be honest about ourselves to date, we have mortgaged the future and virtually said it would never be any different. This is working atheism. This bows God out. This gives Him no connection of faith by which He can reach us at all except in superficial ways to repeat impressions already made. We know that, if we would let go more deeply, and allow ourselves to be more often immersed in the stream of the Holy Spirit, our pious inaction and pseudo-spiritual humility would give way to radiant living and a joyous, God-centered assurance.

We say glibly that we must be converted more than once. This is true. But it tends to let us off the hook of making somewhere at some time as deep a decision as we know how to make. At its heart, this means the opening up of our lives to the light and will of God—it involves a kind of death as the beginning of new life. It should involve our own commitment to whatever is our part in building His Kingdom in the world. And it must involve some human particulars, also: a dishonesty to clear up, a broken relation to be repaired, a habit that must begin to be broken. We may need someone else with whom to talk all this out, and to be like a witness when we seal up the decision with God. The universal necessity for this kind of commitment is the answer to people who say, with supreme self-satisfaction, "I was brought up in the Church, and need no conversion." These are the lineal descendants of the Pharisees, and are Pharisees themselves . . . "*Them*selves," or "*our*selves"—which?

The growth and nourishment which must follow immediately upon this fresh decision will involve both old and new factors. We shall have to revitalize what we already know and have, and we shall have to learn a lot we do not know and have. Under the impulse of a deep commitment, all those "means of grace" that may have been familiar for years in the idea, come to life and offer us help. A person beginning to be changed seeks avidly the words of the Scripture because now he is committed to the life set forth there. He wants to work and worship with God's people in and through the Church. He will pray with increasing frequency and power. He looks for every help he can find, through Sacraments, books, and fellowship. How often do we hear ministers urge people to make use of these things, whereas if they went for the conversion which comes first, the people would not need to be urged to read their Bibles or pray or come to Church or make their Communions. These people are still *out of the life*—how can they be expected to act or react as if they were in it? But, once in the life, once in the stream of the Spirit, it is all too good to lose. They want more. Only spiritually eager people will either do anything about their private spiritual discipline, or their relation to the Church. Once let them catch a vision of themselves as part of a great awakening under the Holy Spirit, and they will know how badly they need the helps that Christ has provided through His Church and His Book.

There are three fields where our new start will be felt.

The first is in our homes. The homes where husband and wife are committed to Christ and to His work in the world are the healthiest and happiest homes I ever see. In them God is a constant factor. Children grow up, not amid perfection, but with parents who are obviously concerned to let God rule their lives and their homes as much as possible. There will be failures in this, failures in love and in patience sometimes. A Christian home is not one in which the relationships are perfect—I know none such—but one in which the imperfections and failures are acknowledged and where problems are worked out in prayer and obedience to the light God sends. In such homes there is great freedom for people to say what they think and express what they feel. There is not the repression of law imposed by one or both of the parents on the children, nor by somebody's temper or tears on everybody. People are allowed to grow up, to make mistakes, to be themselves, to laugh, to live through difficult crises or periods with privacy if they want it, with help if they want that. Where there is the free control of the Spirit, there will not need to be the cramping control of one upon another. "Where the Spirit of the Lord is there is liberty," and there is also a certain kind of rather indefinable order. Each one in touch with the Spirit, and the Spirit in and over all—that is something of the flavor of homes that illustrate and spread the awakening of the Spirit.

The second is in our daily work. We shall lose the sense that this is a necessary grind in order to provide a livelihood, and begin seeing it as our corner of the Kingdom. I shall never forget the first days of Ralston Young's new life: how was he to express this, carrying bags in Grand Central Station? First he caught the spirit of other men who were seeing in their jobs a spiritual opportunity, not just a material necessity. Then he began thinking of all the people he met day after day; and it came to him that he must "carry their burdens as well as their bags." Quietly and under the Spirit this began to happen, till he started calling the station his "cathedral," and chaffing me by saying, "A lot more people go through my cathedral than go through your church!" And for more than sixteen years his ministry has continued in that emporium of travel. I cannot think of a more difficult field, with people in a hurry all the time; but that is where his life is set, and that is where he wins people for Christ. Each of us must find his own niche in the world, God's place for him—usually the place where we are until or unless we are being urged by the Spirit to go somewhere else. But this niche is not like a corner in a museum where a statue stands: it is like a position a soldier must defend in the front line of a war.

The third field is our parish church. There will be some of us going along with the program as the minister and his board outline it, gladly making our own contribution to it. With full identification with them, we may have other contributions to make. There may be no such thing as a small group in the parish, for prayer or for the exchange of experience or for training. The confidence of the minister must be won if a group is to be started in the parish. It may be well to meet somewhere else than in a church, partly because of its being more congenial to some outsiders, partly because a group should often be "ecumenical" and inclusive of people from different churches. But every local church needs to see its own life and work related, not only to community problems, or to its own denomination, but to the Church-at-Large, the whole work of the Kingdom. We lose our vision when we are too preoccupied with the local scene. We shall only keep mindful of the big picture as individuals, groups, boards, guilds, as well as clergy learn more of the Spirit's power and guidance. We must all learn to say no to the less important claims in order that we may say yes to those we know to have our names written on them. Bishop Pardue, of Pittsburgh, said to me, "I am convinced the only thing to do is to find your own objective, be polite, and work to produce fruits." A streamlined aim like that would set every parish church far ahead of where it is.

If our lives are to be geared to the Spirit, we shall emphasize organisms, not organizations; relationships, not arrangements; events, not mechanics; stories, not ideas; people, and not things.

We must be both aware of, and grateful for, the many people and places and events in which the Holy Spirit is really at work, even if not in the customary, orthodox fashion. In the attempt to keep our beliefs pure, to reverence our Church, to acknowledge the inspiration of our Scriptures, we have narrowed the area in which we think He is to be found. This does not do Him service: this separates Him still further from the present-day world. One can name without long thought a dozen men and women, and as many causes or events in our day, where He is present, though perhaps not articulately so. They may be people and enterprises with which technical religion is in no way connected. If we expect to find an avowed evangelism or the outward lingo of religion in these places, we shall ask the impossible. But all things are His. If we do not recognize the Holy Spirit in anything but a surplice or Geneva gown, in any language but that of full-blown religion, in any book but one with a black leather cover, in any words but a sermon or a church resolution, in any cause that is not directly sponsored by the Church, we shall fail to recognize many an ally in the world-wide awakening that we need. So much of what the churches do and sponsor has lost all taste for the outsider. We shall need the dimension of depth in our convictions, but the dimension of breadth in our sympathies. These are hard to come by, but we must seek them.

This will have to extend to our language also. The Quakers used many phrases to denote the presence of the Holy Spirit: the

Light, the Seed, the Christ Within, the Spirit, That of God in man, etc. Fresh and current experience will clothe itself with fresh and current language. When a familiar phrase becomes threadbare, or too much associated with a particular group or method, let it be discarded and a fresh one take its place. I wish we could blank out most of the language of religion, and make people say what they mean in simple, familiar, homespun words. In seeking to be dignified, we become pompous. In trying to be theologically correct, we become obscure. The words that are meant to reveal the truth serve to conceal it instead. Let us get in the habit of talking about the experiences of religion with complete naturalness.

We must have observed by now that religion which is alive today is rather a network of relationships than a system of organizations. The old denominational and even theological divisions are a little shopworn now; but the distinction between those who live in an increasingly wide-flung fellowship of the Spirit, and those who function only through organizations, is a terribly valid one. We ought first to seek, with people, the establishment of a relationship which has the Holy Spirit for the Third Party all the time, rather than just the doing of business with them, even if it is the Lord's business. For all the increase in population and in the number of people some of us are thrown into contact with, a growing impersonalness infests our society. It may yet be that only the God-motivated people can keep us even human in this mechanistic age. It takes time, ingenuity, even physical and emotional energy, to give ourselves to people; but we must do it. Start reaching out with caring and concern. Not long ago I wrote a man I scarcely knew, but who was in trouble. He came to see me. I listened to him, shared with him, later prayed with him. He writes, "The fellowship provided me with an infusion of faith and courage, coming from one who would listen and understand. I have done more business in the past ten days than I had in the previous two months. Much better than that, though, are the experiences I have had talking with various people about faith. The most difficult man in our office came to me with his problems and I think before long he will find Christ."

This reminds us that we must cease from splitting life down the middle into religious and secular. The concern which went into this man helped deepen his relation to God, but it showed up at the level of a job by which to support himself and his family. We must pray earnestly to the Holy Spirit to guide and use us at the daily work level. Surely God is more interested in life than in religion! That means the whole of life, not the spiritual part of it only. In this world we know nothing of a spirit apart from a body. The life, the spirit, should control the body, but the two are found together. Church on Sunday, making money from Monday till Saturday, must give way to a faith that receives new impetus on Sundays, or from private prayer, but keeps pouring itself out all through the week in every relationship. Of course this is going to build greater confidence and trust, and lead to possibly more business; but we must remember that at times the Spirit will lead us to take moral stands that will lessen the flow of success and income. It is a fake spirituality which thinks God can never help people make a sale; and it is also a fake practicality which thinks He must always do it. We must pray and let Him work. All of life is His, and He wants to make use of it for His glory.

Let us beware of fanaticism. Faith in the Holy Spirit, even the beginnings of a true experience of Him, can be the occasion for the old ego to reassert itself. We can think we are guided in directions which prove in the end to be false, and we can be pushed by the uprush of subconscious energies in directions that manifest more of self than of God. Moreover, some people —maybe most people—have quirks of temperament or personality that might be used by God if they were yielded to Him, but which unyielded can make them objectionable. There is a type of starry-eyed religious person that makes me want to run when I see him coming. Whole groups of people can fall under some kind of group spell that is a very deceptive counterfeit for "the fellowship of the Holy Spirit," and which may carry them in false paths. If we are of such temperaments, let us ask God's help in guarding against their running away with us.

But spiritual wildness and excess are not the problem of most people. As Father Bull said years ago, "Delirious emotionalism is not the chief peril of the English clergy." It is not ours, either. Our peril is a struggling, uninspired, lackluster, joyless performance of old religious routines. St. Paul had to call back his Corinthian Christians from their excesses by saying, ". . . all things should be done decently and in order" (I Cor. 14:40, RSV). This is good counsel for threatened fanaticism: it is poor counsel for those who make an idol of conventionality. God can use much that is found in the Church, but some of it is useless lumber. So much of what goes on in the Church lacks fire, inspiration, vitality, and contagion. Some of our people might as well be the Ephesians who have "not so much as heard whether there be any Holy Spirit" (Acts 19:2). But others are seeking, dissatisfied, hungry for something they are missing. Many have left us and gone to find it in the more primitive sects and more will go unless we help them find the Holy Spirit in some measure as they knew Him in the Early Church. There is a great deal of uneasiness in the most spiritual of our people in the Church, a great deal of hopelessness in people round about us on the outside. The one answer for them both is a fresh descent of the Holy Spirit upon the Church and moving out into the world.

We can no more will this than we can organize it. There is a great mystery about the Holy Spirit. He comes when He will, He goes when He will. God seems to have an economy concerning the Holy Spirit. He will sometimes break through the most pedestrian of routines, and He will sometimes come only in fire and great glory. He is felt in vast church assemblies at times, and He is seen in obscure village churches and unknown people in out-of-the-way places. He can be with us one minute, and far from us the next, because we have disobeyed Him. Yet human sin does not seem to explain all the reason for His withdrawals. We cannot fathom Him, being Himself God.

But we can know that He is our great need and our great hope. We can begin seeking and finding some of those experiences which are a kind of contemporary embodiment and incarnation of what Jesus came into the world to bring, and of which the Holy Spirit is the Instigator and Inspirer. We can ask Him to take from us the littleness and the self-centeredness that bind us. We can keep praying to be lifted by Him into that stream of grace and love and power which is His life in the world. Instead of the dark world of our forebodings and fears, we might see a bright world of His making.

Everything depends on Him, except the obedience He expects from us. That depends on us alone.